15/6/99.

To: Arric

Scott Balson

One Voice, Many Issues

by

Scott Balson

May 1999

First printing: May 1999

Published by: Interactive Presentations Pty Ltd
Typeset and cover design: Global Web Builders

ISBN 0-646-37387-0

One Voice, Many Issues

"What makes a state sovereign," Rabkin writes, ***"is that it need answer to no outside authority. For us, sovereignty means the primacy of our own Constitution. The people of the United States, by their own sovereign authority, have made the Constitution supreme over the government, and no outside agreement can challenge that supremacy."***

Global treaties and agreements are a direct threat to every Australian citizen. As Rabkin states they are an assault on our right to raise and educate our children as we see fit. They are an attack on our ownership of private property. They are an attack on our sovereignty and everything that we hold dear. They are an attack on the Australian standard of living because their goal is to steal Australian wealth and give it to the multinationals. Worse still, in the long term the road of globalisation will lead to a single global government where corporations not people rule the world.

The traitor in our midst peddling these treaties as right and "unstoppable" is the Australian media. Sadly, their compliant partners are the major parties who represent us in government.

"...with every multilateral treaty or bargain; every adhesion to bodies such as the United Nations or General Agreement on Tariffs and Trade; every agreement on the international trading regime, on international co-ordination and standards on human rights and the environment, or the rights of indigenous peoples, or racial, sexual, or other discrimination; on international property rights or cultural co-operation; with every convention of the International Labour Organisation signed – there has been not only the cessation of new heads of power for the Commonwealth, but a cessation of power to interfere in and legislate for Australia to the various international communities of signatories and organisations..."

P.P. McGuiness, The Australian, 22nd March 1994

Foreword:

This book is a natural progression from the author's earlier expose on the media barons and mainstream political parties in Australia. *"Murder by Media, Death of Democracy in Australia"*, launched in January 1999[1].

The Queensland Independent, published by the University of Queensland's Department of Journalism says, ***"He has done this brilliantly. The level of research that has gone into producing this book*** *("Murder by Media")* ***is what makes it. Far from just crying wolf, Scott Balson has gone through the village with photographs. His views are supported, his assertions are researched, and so his attacks are grounded."***

Unlike *"Murder by Media"* this book is a layman's guide to seventeen key issues facing all Australians today and in the future. These issues are centered around the concerted push by the major political parties and the media for Australia to embrace *"globalisation"*, which we are told is *"unstoppable"*.

The book also looks at political correctness in all its ugly forms, as well as the unsavoury impact that the new world order is having on Australian society.

It is now up to all thinking and informed Australians to play a role in bringing Australia back from the brink.

This book details why the major parties can no longer be trusted to do what is right for the people of Australia. It will take a concerted effort by minor political parties and groups like Pauline Hanson's One Nation, Australia First, and Independents working together with a single-minded common goal.

This goal must be the saving of Australia from the new world order – which is waiting expectantly in the wings.

This political alliance must succeed if it is to create a confusing, moving target that the media will find hard to tag and vilify. It will provide the political foundation for a new Australia free of the social erosion taking place under our noses today.

---

[1] "Murder by Media, Death of Democracy in Australia" can be ordered on-line (http://members.tripod.com/balson/order.htm) or by sending a payment of Au$27 (includes postage and handling) to: S Balson, P.O. Box 11, Mt Crosby News, QLD 4306.

One Voice, Many Issues

It's easy, perhaps to die for a dream
With banners unfurled - and be forgiving!
It's the hardest part to follow the gleam
When scorned by the world - and go on living!

Myra Brooks Welch

First published in Australia by Interactive Presentations Pty Ltd

First Edition (1999). Release 1.0 – May 1999

ISBN 0-646-37387-0

One voice

The past – "Colonisation"

I lived in Colonial Africa in the 1950s and early 60s. I had a remarkable childhood – a proverbial *"white"* Lord of the Manor. I did not think twice about the plight of the black Africans who cooked my family's meals or toiled in the garden or laboured with the house cleaning. Yes, we had three *"servants"* – we could afford them because they were paid little and demanded nothing but food with which to feed their family. In our privileged role we saw ourselves as giving them an opportunity to live a better life.

Most Africans in the little town of Iringa in Tanzania lived in absolute poverty. It was nothing unusual to walk through the dusty lanes that traversed the squalid village market and see destitute mothers begging for a few cents with which to feed their dirty, half-dressed children who stared blankly through the heat - oblivious of the normal childhood wonders of life around them.

The poverty of the people was so absolute that I, as a young boy, had grown to accept that this was the fate of the black African and that somehow I deserved to have a different path along life's road. Despite the poverty the colonial power provided an element of stability that many indigenous tribes had not enjoyed before. This, we believed, made our act of Colonial occupation acceptable.

Of course Colonisation by foreign government as we knew it in those days is all but dead today. During the 1960s and 1970s countries throughout Africa and the rest of the world were released from the shackles of rule by foreign governments. The European powers were forced to release their colonies by the US and banks as part of war-debt underwriting following World War II.

They had, we were told, sought and achieved independence. However, all that they had achieved in reality was a shift of dependence under a far worse tyranny.

Throughout modern times the power had been traditionally in the hands of the people through the governments of powerful European governments. As rulers over the colonies these governments encouraged their citizens to settle in their foreign lands and to exploit the mineral wealth and to enjoy the privileged lifestyle that my family once enjoyed. The shift of dependence appeared with profit driven multinationals like BP Oil in the Congo and the South African based De Beers diamond mines in Angola. They soon replacing the Colonial power vacuum. While lengthy and debilitating civil wars were being fought in Angola the diamond mines operated in a surreal environment where they were somehow isolated from the death and destruction just outside their fence lines.

The colonial powers, with all their failings, had ensured stability and protection for the people in their colonies. Today the new world order is establishing a new and far more destructive agenda.

During this time of change the multinationals have entrenched their positions of exploitation in tiny geographic cells in third world countries like the Congo. They have fed the greed of the local power-base through Swiss bank accounts while ripping the inherent wealth from the ground. If trouble arises they are protected by a new global policeman – the UN. The starving African populations just outside the barbed wire fences protecting the assets of these foreign powers have been, at best, ignored or at worst driven away.

In other third world countries where there is nothing of value to exploit the fate of the people has been even worse as they are left to fend for themselves as their country is devastated by falling standards of living, tribal warfare/multiculturalism and a rapidly increasing population. A human time-bomb – worse still, this global cancer is unchecked and has now infected Australia.

The present – "globalisation"

My parents left East Africa following independence. The colonial infrastructure was stripped away and quickly replaced with a mentality of corruption, violence and power outlined above.

We live in an age in which traditional European colonial superpowers have been successfully replaced by massive multinational companies with spending power far exceeding all but the wealthiest nations of the world.

The first cancer spots have appeared in Australia – not a third world country yet but taking backward steps all the time... The fate of the peoples in Brazil is our crystal ball into the future because their lurch back into poverty and dependence mirrors the track we are currently taking.

When I came to Australia, the *"lucky country"*, in 1986 I found myself in a sovereign country lurching towards a position of subservience to the money powers in Wall Street. This is where the heart of the new world order can be traced.

I could sense a clear change in my role in this new age. Where I had once been the *"lord of the manor"* I could see that, even in

Australia, that the mainstream population with its generally high standard of living, was quickly becoming the *"servant"* of the new Colonial powers under the guise of a global level playing field.

Now in 1999 Australia has arrived at the cross-roads. The country's financial indebtedness, the effective foreign control of its four big banks, the concentration of the media as well as the drive by the new masters, the multinationals, for this unlevel *"level playing field"* have all played a part in destroying the social fabric and the standards of living many Australians once enjoyed.

The reality of inner Sydney at night now brings back clear memories of my youth in colonial Africa. Homeless teenage children can be seen walking the streets, some even beg, thousands of teenagers sell their bodies in prostitution to survive. Theft, crime, drugs and assaults are commonplace as the *"lucky country"* loses its innocence. These are the first symptoms of social decay under the new world order. The poor and displaced currently get some social security support from the government but this will be removed under the new economic rationalist regime – with government policy dictated by foreign interests. The glitz and glamour of the American soap programmes on television give the lie to the fact that millions of their citizens live below the poverty line in ghettos and squalor reminiscent of what I experienced in Africa in the 1950s and 60s.

I wrote this book to alert Australians, and hopefully politicians to some of the key issues which we should be addressing if we are to come back from the brink.

But perhaps it is already too late.

Today's *"level playing field"* is all about the exclusion of the population from decision making; the raping and pillaging of foreign lands under the guise of globalisation and the entrenchment of a world government run by big business, for big business. It matters not if the country be the Congo or Australia, the people black or white, the new world order does not discriminate against race or religion its agenda has one single goal – global control by corporations.

The future – "corporate world government"

If it is too late then it is only fair that I paint a picture of what the new world order has got planned for us.

Globalisation is a battle rarely fought with arms and soldiers, this is a battle where several non-military forces work together to achieve a common aim in a world where a small number of multinational companies will rule the world. They have already effectively replaced the Colonial governments in many poor countries and are now hauling in bigger catches – like Australia.

The quantum shift between the poverty that I witnessed as a privileged child under Colonialism is political stability – this will collapse – even in the new Australia. Political correctness and multiculturalism will come back to haunt and divide us.

The great divide will be between the extremely wealthy and the poor - the haves and the have nots. The transition will be complete. My youthful memories of colonial Africa recall one harsh reality – there was no middle class, neither will there be one in Australia.

The new *"servants"* will be the Australian worker earning wages below the poverty line, and serving the new breed of elite in a manner not dissimilar to that of my childhood memories.

In April 1999 I visited the Hilton Hotel in Brisbane. Several years ago the staff had been made up of men and women in their 40s... with a sprinkling of younger people taking up some junior roles.

Today most staff in the *"hospitality industry"* are teenagers working on youth wages or *"work experience"*. The wages of just $5.60 per hour, often irrespective of the day or time at which many work, are a long shot from the $1 per day earned by Vietnamese workers but the gap has already reduced dramatically.

The new *"Colonial"* masters waiting in the wings are the foreign business executives and a small number of wealthy Australians who will wander the globe as the new lords of the global manor. They already pay little or no tax – that burden is left to those who can least afford it.

Tragically, the road we are on is shared by other countries like Canada, Japan, the UK, US and South Africa. In the longer term we are all destined to be come part of a new world government with its heart at the United Nations and the power base in the boardroom.

The elite in the US already see themselves as the *"global policeman"* thinking nothing of launching attacks on sovereign nations like Serbia and Iraq with impunity. President Clinton openly talks of *"protecting US (big business) interests"* when justifying these attacks.

Harry Rankin, Q.C., lifetime Bencher of The Law Society of British Columbia wrote in April 1999[2]: *In my naivete I thought a*

[2] http://www.gwb.com.au/gwb/news/multi/kosovo5.htm

great new world loomed on the horizon. Instead, we have descended to an alliance of the lickspittle Tony Blair and the Social Democrats of the world grovelling and slobbering before that great "Statesman" Clinton, all in a mad subservience to the New World Order euphemistically named "Globalization". It is a submission to the money men, the new fascist elite, who are imposing their will on the people of the world.

While the new world order controlled media would have us believe that these massive shows of force are justified for *"humanitarian"* reasons just a cursory look under the covers reveals a very different agenda.

Consider the state of Israel which was founded on the brutal *"ethnic cleansing"* of 700,000 Palestinians who were forced into neighbouring countries as refugees. A country where Palestinians are, even today, evicted from their homes to allow the Jewish state to expand – yet no NATO or UN intervention.

or the Sudan where thousands of Christians have been enslaved and thousands killed, and they continue to be enslaved / killed with impunity by Islamic people – yet the UN takes no action.

Perhaps the most stark example of what I am suggesting is the conflicting manner in which the UN responded to an attack on oil-rich Kuwait by Iraq when compared to its lack of interest in protecting the Kurds in the barren lands to the north. The difference was the interests of the multinationals and their oil fields.

One Voice:

The only option available to Australian people today is to understand the hidden agenda that underlie the sometimes illogical decisions being taken by our government.

Knowledge is power. Unfortunately most politicians are so caught up in their careers and vote catching that they do not spend time looking at or understanding the issues effecting our nation.

This book is but one voice which attempts to address and explain these issues in layman's terms.

May it fall on many ears and open the minds of the people to the pitfalls that we have already fallen into and those that lie ahead.

I do not have the answers, even though I offer solutions to the issues. What I do offer readers is the truth that for our children's sakes we must understand what foreign powers have in store for this country because our political leaders are lost in the wilderness.

Colonisation of Australia by Corporations

External influencing factors:

- United Nations, World Trade Organisation, OECD, World Bank, IMF, etc. the backbone of globalisation
- Secret international trade and banking agreements like Lima, MAI, FSIA, MIGA, GATT etc..
- Trade tariff reduction
- Deregulation

End result – foreign ownership and control of Australia's assets.

The "globalist agenda" go-betweens:

- Media: promoting the globalist and political correctness agenda
- Major parties: working with and funded by big business. Underwritten by the two party system

Internal influencing factors:

- Political correctness and Multiculturalism
- Shifting the line in the sand in accepted moral standards
- Shifting of tax burden
- Hilmer Report – privatisation of public assets
- Two party system (compulsory preferential voting)
- The Republic Debate

End result – Break down of political stability, increasing unemployment and foreign control.

Issue Briefings:

Only the issues that I consider to be the key areas where Australia has or is currently coming apart at the seams are covered in this book. Select any of the issues listed below to get a better understanding of just how Australia is being sabotaged from within.

Do not make the mistake of looking at each issue in isolation, because they are all part of the same. They all lead our children to a world under corporate rule where the lucky will have "Mcjobs" - a modern day comparison to those enjoyed by my parent's servants while the rest will be begging in the streets in a new world order without a social conscience.

Chapter 1
Globalisation And The MAI

Background:

For corporations to rule the world they have to encourage sovereign countries to accept new secretive laws which pass the traditional pillars of sovereignty and independence from the people to them. These include the privatisation of public utilities, like Telstra, Qantas and the Commonwealth Bank, legal tax avoidance schemes to maximise profits, and the unrestricted flow of capital to facilitate unfettered globalisation.

On December 1, 1997, Foreign Minister Alexander Downer addressed journalists at the Canberra Press Club, confirming that the Howard government was committed to *"globalising"* Australia. *"We all fall into one of two camps",* Downer said. *"You are either a globaphobe or a globaphile.*

"The globaphobes among us seek to relive the past, not confront the future".

"Opposing globalism will shut us off from fast changing technology, from rising living standards, from new and more interesting jobs," Downer said.

Downer failed to realise that most Australians today are still unaware just what *"globalisation"* actually means.

Globalisation simply means *"political and economic integration"*. The social conscience, as we know it, will be a thing of the past when this occurs – in many key areas, such as banking, it already is. The all-powerful financial boardrooms in Wall Street are already powerful behind the scene manipulators in comparatively small countries like Australia. Where Australians once voted as a people on the direction that they wanted their country to move this democratic right is being replaced by powerful men or women sitting around a boardroom table on Wall Street in New York, or London. Australia as we know it today is regressing to a new level of unconscionable colonialism. If unchecked, these men and women will have the financial clout to determine everything that happens in you and your children's day to day life from the interest rates that they pay on their mortgage to the price of a bus ticket. Governments will be reduced to nothing more than watchdogs who manage rather than support the people.

Globalisation and the MAI

Globalisation is about countries relinquishing, bit by bit, their economic sovereignty, their economic assets and public utilities, together with their political, legal, and cultural sovereignty to internationalist and big business control. The resultant *'globalised'* world is to consist not of independent nations, but of interdependent member states of a global order under one world government. This world government is embodied in the United Nations (UN) and its global big business partners like the World Trade Organisation (WTO), the International Monetary Fund (IMF), and the Organisation for Economic Co-operation and Development (OECD).

The trend breaks every democratic rule in the book. Hans Kohn, in the book *'Nationalism: Its Meaning and History'* states (p.9*), "A deep attachment to one's native soil, to local traditions and to established territorial authority has existed in varying strengths throughout* history[3]."

Morris Ginsberg writing on the diversity of morals says, *"The essential characteristic of the nation is the sentiment of unity. In this sense nationalism must be very ancient, since there must always have existed groups conscious of their unity.[4]"*

The Fontana Dictionary of Modern Thought says: *"Despite the rival claims of class war on the one hand and internationalism on the other, nationalism as a mass emotion has been the most powerful political force in the history of the world.[5]"*

Globalisation is the antithesis of this *"nationalism"*. That is why this perfectly normal human sentiment is treated as an anathema by the media.

The Multilateral Agreement on Investment (or MAI) epitomises the secret march towards world government through international treaties which forge *"globalisation"*.

This is how Graham Strachan[6] sums up globalisation:

"A competitive market is a clearly defined thing: a market of potentially unlimited competitors, competing on more or less an equal footing, in a market which newcomers can freely enter, and in which none can control price [Adam Smith, 'The Wealth of Nations']. Something like it probably existed for a while in Britain

---

[3] Hans Kohn, 'Nationalism: Its Meaning and History' (1965).

[4] Morris Ginsberg, 'On the Diversity of Morals' (1962), p.244.

[5] The Fontana Dictionary of Modern Thought, 2nd Edition, 1988.

[6] Author of "Globalisation: Demise of the Australian nation".

during the Industrial Revolution, but once big business came on the scene from around 1870 onwards, [Parkinson, 'The Rise of Big Business'], the truly competitive market disappeared and has never been seen since.

"Why? Because big business bought up or destroyed smaller competitors in the marketplace and produced a situation called oligopoly....market control by a few large firms, with weaker competitors struggling to survive on the periphery. Oligopoly was not a competitive market, and until the advent of economic rationalism nobody seriously suggested that it was. Oligopoly was regarded as a symptom of market failure, only marginally better than outright monopoly [see Galbraith, 'American Capitalism']."

The above extract from one of Graham Strachan's articles on globalisation[7] reflects what many of us see but do not understand - the growing foreign ownership of Australians assets and businesses.

This includes the seemingly endless privatisation of public assets such as electricity, Telstra, Qantas, the Commonwealth Bank, water and gas utilities, transport and even our prisons.

The Australian manufacturing industry is under assault. In 1961 27.5% of Australians were employed in this industry area, but by 1996 that figure had dropped to 12.9%, less than half. The jobs are going to countries like Vietnam where the pay can be as low as $1 per day. The government's enthusiastic removal of tariff protection has forced manufacturers to either move offshore to where the cheaper labour is or go broke. We then import goods once manufactured here exacerbating our foreign debt problems.

These are visible signs of *"globalisation"*. We see them reported on in the daily paper, without explanation or concern as we are told the *"inevitable"* is happening.

For example when *"the (once) big Australian"* BHP closed its steel mills in Newcastle at the cost of thousands of Australian jobs it moved that employment opportunity to Indonesia where labour costs and benefits were a quantum leap lower. The added bonus for BHP in Indonesia was that the labour union problems that the company faced in Australia when trying to *"increase productivity"* or *"reduce labour costs"* would be a thing of the past because of the high level of unemployment and abject poverty in that country.

---

[7] http://www.gwb.com.au/gwb/news/economic/130299.htm article headed: "Globaphilia and Economic Blindness"

Globalisation and the MAI

The MAI was to be one of the nails in the coffin of sovereignty as we understand it. In the words of Renato Ruggerio, Director General of the WTO, *"We are writing the constitution of a single Global Economy (through the MAI)."*

The negotiation of the agreement commenced under Labor in 1995, and was continued unquestioned under the current Coalition government.

There should be absolutely no doubt in anybody's mind that the negotiations on the MAI were conducted between senior Australian bureaucrats, big business interests in this country and the OECD countries to the total exclusion of the general population – those who would be most effected by its implementation.

The Courier-Mail reported at the time the MAI was exposed by Pauline Hanson (January 1998):

...Peak industry groups support the proposed agreement arguing that it will remove restraints on international capital flows and make the process more open.

Australian Chamber of Commerce and Industry chief executive Mark Patterson said yesterday ***that industry had been consulted extensively on the agreement.***

He said Ms Hanson's concerns were unfounded.

The much heralded comment *"that the MAI would never be allowed to happen on this basis (where sovereignty is challenged)"* should be considered in light of the Lima agreement. This secret non-binding agreement gave the ground rules for globalisation and its implementation, including the movement of industry and manufacturing from Australia to Asia through the removal of tariff protection. Despite the agreement being non-binding, Australia honours it today. Australia's signing of little-known binding WTO treaties like the Financial Services Industry Agreement (FSIA) Australian banks have become foreign owned.

Shortly after the MAI was exposed by Pauline Hanson, a lone voice in Parliament, the media and the Coalition government went into damage control establishing the Joint Standing Committee on Treaties (JSCT) with Liberal MP, Bill Taylor as its Chairman. Soon after the JSCT was established Taylor wrote in *The Courier-Mail*:

The Federal Government has not signed anything yet; there is no secret government deal done with shadowy United Nations figures in the OECD in Paris; the matter has been referred to the joint standing committee on treaties (which I chair) by the Minister for

Foreign Affairs for review; and public views were invited in all capital city newspapers on March 14.

A few months later the committee's own findings contradicted Taylor's claims saying there were some *"serious and legitimate concerns"* being raised about Australia's involvement in this *"secretive and undemocratic treaty aimed at opening our doors to big business"*.

The contradiction became irrelevant when the Coalition Government called a federal election for 3rd October 1998. The JSCT, like all federally appointed committees, was stood down after the announcement. Less than three weeks after the federal election senior bureaucrats from Treasury were back in Paris working for the MAI to proceed despite the committee's findings.

It was only the dissent of France and the US just days before the critical October 22nd meeting that stopped the MAI being ratified. France objected on the grounds of protecting her culture. The US argued that the proposed watered down MAI *did not provide enough incentive for their big banks.* This is documented on the OECD website on the Internet[8]. Australia's treasury bureaucrats were ready to sign the MAI – despite the concerns raised by the JSCT and the public statements by politicians that *"it would not be allowed to proceed"*.

More seriously, no Australian paper questioned Australia's decision to let the treaty proceed after the committee's findings against participation had been published.

The agenda?

The winners under an MAI would have been the Packer and Murdoch media empires as the *"level playing field"* envisaged under it would have outlawed Australia's media ownership laws. The losers would have been the Australian population.

In a front page article on the 3rd of November 1998 *The Australian* said[9]:

A global treaty that would have eased controls on foreign investment has collapsed handing the Howard Government a fillip in its bid to soften its economic rationalist image and neutralise the One Nation threat.

Assistant treasurer Rod Kemp said yesterday the three-year long negotiations on a Multilateral Agreement on Investment (MAI)

---

[8] http://www.oecd.org/daf/cmis/mai/maindex.htm

[9] See: http://www.gwb.com.au/gwb/news/498/0311.html

broke down under the weight of concerns among some industrialised nations, including Australia.

One Nation had been able to exploit nationalist sentiments by staunchly opposing the agreement in line with its anti-foreign investment stance.

In March 1999 the JSCT came out with its final and official Conclusions and Recommendations which showed how uninformed reporters like Peter Charlton and politicians like Kim Beazley had been proven to be in their public statements about the MAI.

Just one of many points made by the JSCT states, *"Had the draft MAI proceeded, there would have been impacts on Australia. Treaties can involve agreeing to limitations on national power or activity for a perceived larger good. Many of the concerns about the likely impact of the draft Agreement on Australian sovereignty were over-stated. They were often linked with objections to what was seen as the secret way in which negotiations were conducted"*.

The JSCT final report was completely ignored by the mainstream media. A chilling thought when one considers the long term impact that the MAI promised to deliver to the population.

There are many other issues linked to globalisation which are covered in this book. They should not be seen in isolation but be identified as parts of a big jigsaw puzzle which if allowed to be completed will leave Australian's as slaves to foreign ownership.

The issues:

The MAI's purpose was to transfer key elements of power and control away from citizens and their democratically elected representatives to the world's largest multinationals - with no strings attached. The major issue was the secrecy which enveloped the negotiations. Only the "big business" club in Australia were in on the deal – setting up the parameters for the de-facto grab on the sovereignty of states around the world.

The other issues relevant to the MAI include:

- Australian governments, whether federal, state or local, would not be able to favour local business over foreigners.
- Any performance requirements for multinationals, such as creating jobs for Australians, using local components, or loyalty to Australia, would not be allowed.

- Australia would not be able to stop multinationals from importing foreign workers and their families into our country.
- Multinationals would be able to sue all three levels of Australian government for any infringements of the rights given to them by the agreement - it would be the Australian taxpayers who would pay the legal costs and damages compensation.
- Temporary exemptions to the *"level playing field"* such as media ownership would have to be wound back after a few years – in a 20 year binding agreement.

It is important to understand that the MAI was not about trade, it was all about power and control over Australia's sovereignty.

The agreement was designed to impose tight restrictions on what Australia could do when regulating its own economy. For example, we would no longer be able to attach conditions to, or limit the extent of foreign investment and many of our decisions would be made by international bureaucrats and boardrooms in Wall Street.

It would have made it impossible for Australians to run their country for their own interests. The governments, at all levels, would in many respects have been reduced to simple managers and caretakers for foreigners.

If the MAI and the sale of Telstra had gone ahead as Australian bureaucrats had planned in 1998, it would also have resulted in the loss of our telecommunications giant to foreign investors. Under the MAI existing safeguards about foreign ownership would have been challenged in an international court after the first few years of the implementation of the MAI.

What the major parties thought about this issue:

It was Labor's Senator Peter Cook, then Minister for Trade, who represented Australia at the OECD Ministers' conference in May 1995 who agreed to commence MAI negotiations, and it was Labor who oversaw those negotiations between May 1995 and Labor's defeat in March 1996. The MAI negotiations continued uninterrupted under the new Coalition government.

In December 1997 I contacted the major parties about the MAI and was told that they had no understanding of what I was talking about and words to the effect that *"they were not interested anyway"*. When I alerted Ms Hanson to the MAI she had a different perspective and called that now historic press conference.

Globalisation and the MAI

At the time that Ms Hanson raised concerns about the MAI in the press conference on 21st January 1998 the leader of the Labor party, Kim Beazley, was in Hobart at the party's annual convention. When asked about the MAI he said that it was *"good for Australia"*.

The Coalition's official position after her press conference was that Ms Hanson did not know what she was talking about.

Andrew Downer telling a group of businessmen in London after her press conference,

"I have noticed in Australia the sort of campaign that people like Pauline Hanson at the moment are running, saying that by going along with MAI, that means Australia is going to be swamped by a lot of terrible foreigners and the whole of Australia is going to be sold off.

"I think that, first of all, it needs to be understood that this agreement isn't going to lead to any changes in Australia's foreign investment policy.

"But secondly Australia has an interest in seeing a more liberal global investment regime.

"And the MAI also will lead to a more liberal global investment regime, although we will still be able to have the restrictions on the sensitive sectors that we currently have in Australia."

The Australian Democrats and Greens supported Ms Hanson's view on the MAI and the on-line *"Stop MAI"* coalition was formed.

How the media have reported on this issue:

The mainstream media report globalisation as *"good for Australia"* and *"unstoppable"* while the reverse is more likely t be true for most Australian people – a haunting thought when yc consider what Senator Bob McMullan said when signing the FSI and its now known outcome to the banking industry. *"The financial services agreement will directly benefit Australian banks, insurance companies and securities traders."*

Increasing concern about the MAI grew despite unbalanced reporting by journalists like Peter Charlton (*The Courier-Mail*'s national affairs editor) who wrote:

Globalisation and the MAI

The MAI, as the questions and answers on this page illustrate[10]*, is an eminently sensible objective for developed nations seeking to level the investment playing field.*

Yet negotiations over the past 30 months have produced some vehement opposition overseas and an odd alliance in Australia of Pauline Hanson's One Nation and the Democrats.

And:

Her (Ms Hanson's) objections are ill-informed, illogical, not based on fact and hysterically outlandish - are typical of other MAI critics, most notably in Canada, which has long had an ambivalent attitude towards foreign direct investment, particularly from big-brother United States. Groups in Canada opposed the North American Free Trade Agreement or NAFTA; MAI's critics claim it is 'NAFTA on steroids'.

Charlton's comments were typical of the Murdoch press which wanted the MAI to be allowed to proceed. It has got to be recognised that the MAI provided a legal vehicle for Packer and Murdoch to override Australian restrictions on media ownership.

Is there a solution:

The MAI has been put on hold in the OECD with negotiations on a similar treaty currently being formulated through the WTO.

Globalisation continues to be forced upon Australians through the subservience of the Australian government.

The only way in which Australians can ensure that no MAI-like treaty is enforced over the population is through politicians becoming more involved with the issue of international treaties. It is not good enough to trust bureaucrats as they often represent big business interests – a committee selected by Australians, not bureaucrats, should be on the front-line of monitoring this area.

On-line research on the MAI:
http://www.gwb.com.au/gwb/news/mai

---

[10] The "questions and answers" Charlton refers to were taken directly from the OECD web site – the proponents of the MAI.

Chapter 2
The FSIA

"We have before us the greatest question that has yet been submitted for our consideration. It involves Australia's national supremacy in finance, and the peace, good government and prosperity of generations yet unborn..."
King O'Mally MHR, speaking on the need for a Commonwealth Bank in the House of Representatives in September 1909.

Background:

Unlike the MAI the FSIA (or Financial Services Industry Agreement) is a *"done deal"*. It is irreversible. The most dramatic impact of the FSIA can be seen in our now foreign-controlled banking industry.

In 1983 Labor's treasurer-elect Paul Keating campaigned on the promise that foreign ownership in Australian banks would not be allowed, saying, *"As to the argument that foreign bank entry will increasingly link Australia to the general instability of the banking system, and lessen Federal government's control over domestic monetary policy, there is no doubt that this must be the case..."*

Yet within a few short years Keating became the most aggressive pro-foreign ownership treasurer in the world – and yes his predictions about the impact on our banking system have since been ratified.

The WTO was rammed through Congress in 1994 as part of the Uruguay Round on the General Agreement on Tariffs and Trade (GATT).

The WTO functions in Geneva as a sort of United Nations of Trade, with a legislature *(where Australia has one out of 117 votes - the same vote as Cuba or Haiti)*. It is a multinational bureaucracy accountable to no one, and *a Supreme Court of trade that ruled against the United States in its first case.*

Australia's entry into the FSIA through the WTO was first signed by then Minister for Trade, Labor's Senator Bob McMullan, on 28th July 1995. A Departmental press release at the time read, in part, *Senator McMullan said the agreement would provide a major boost to the credibility and strength of the multilateral trading system under the WTO. It underlined the importance of the WTO in providing major market opening opportunities for Australian companies.*

"The financial services agreement will directly benefit Australian banks, insurance companies and securities traders," McMullan said.

Yet despite McMullan's rhetoric, the FSIA, an irretrievable international agreement is more virulent than the MAI because it is a financial tool rather than just a trade agreement. If you want to find out how an economy works, the best rule of thumb is *'follow the money'*. In Australia *'the money'* is now foreign controlled.

It is important to note that it was the Labor Party again that bought Australia into the FSIA in the early 1990s. This was a natural progression from the deregulation of the Australian banking industry in 1985 under Keating. His move prompted Euromoney Magazine to proclaim him *"International Treasurer of the Year"*.

The ramifications of the FSIA have never been properly explained to the Australian public – and especially to those most affected – people living in the rural community where hundreds of banks have been closed under the mantle of *"economic rationalism"*.

Simply put, the FSIA is all about allowing the Wall Street financial houses to acquire and control Australian banks.

Negotiations on the FSIA, like negotiations on the MAI, were conducted in great secrecy. The Australian people were not alerted to the massive changes that would take place in our banking industry following its signing.

When the Labor government privatised the Commonwealth Bank in 1991 the Australian people were assured by the politicians that this was in the bank's best interests but, as a safeguard, *the bank would always remain in Australian hands* because this would be enforced in legislation. O'Malley's fairytale *"the people's bank"* was destroyed by this privatisation.

D J Amos in *"The story of the Commonwealth Bank"* writes,

In October 1911 the Labor Government of Mr Andrew Fisher introduced a Bill to provide for the establishment of a Commonwealth Bank, with powers to carry on all the business generally transacted by banks, including that of a savings bank, to be administered under the control of one man (called the "Governor" of the Bank) appointed for seven years. The Bank was to have power to raise a capital of $2 million by the sale of debentures (the security for which was the national credit)..

The FSIA

The intention of the Bill was to make the national credit available to anyone with decent security to offer, to reduce the charges made on overdrafts, bills of exchange, and current accounts by the private banks, to provide a safe investment for savings, and to help in the reduction of public indebtedness...

In June 1912, Sir Denison Miller, a prominent official of the Bank of New South Wales, resigned his position and was appointed Governor of the Commonwealth Bank.

Labor's short-lived *"promise"* that the Commonwealth bank would remain in the *"people's hands"* was broken in December 1997, when the new Coalition government under Treasurer Peter Costello signed amendments to the FSIA which, the WTO website tells us[11]:

Eliminates a prohibition on the acquisition of control of any of Australia's four main banks. Also eliminates a measure which prohibits banks (resident or non-resident) from holding shares in the Commonwealth Bank of Australia and other entities from holding more than five percent of its issued share capital;

Chase Manhattan Nominees moved in with stealth on what was once a publicly owned Australian bank. Today this New York based finance house is one of the Commonwealth Bank's largest shareholders (in the top 5).

It should be noted that all agreements like the FSIA are under the WTO's rules. These state that *"to ensure the conformity of its laws, regulations and administrative procedures with its obligations as provided in the annexed Agreements"*.

WTO (Paragraph 4 of Article XVI). *The "annexed Agreements" include all the substantive multilateral agreements relating to trade in goods and services and agreement on intellectual property rights. This provision thus obligates each member country to revise any national or sub-national laws in conflict with the GATT/WTO. (Korten,[12] 1995).*

---

[11] http://www.wto.org/wto/new/sumfin.htm

[12] David C Korten has an MBA and PhD from Stanford University's Graduate School of Business. He is chair of the board of the Positive Futures Network, president of the People Centered Development Forum, and author of the *book When Corporations Rule the World*. His new book, *The Post-Corporate World*, was released in February 1999.

The FSIA

In other words the laws established by international bureaucrats working for a single world government under big business now supersede laws established to protect Australians.

The WTO has been described by Korten as: *"... a global parliament composed of unelected bureaucrats with the power to amend its own charter without referral to national legislative bodies"*.

New York based Chase Manhattan Nominees, controlled by Rockefeller interests, is today among the top five shareholders in all four of Australia's major banks *(as well as News Corporation).* The ANZ Annual Report reveals that Chase Manhattan Nominees is today the bank's largest shareholder with over 11% of the equity.

With common foreign shareholder control in all four major Australian banks it is quite clear that bank mergers will be the next goal – this will reduce costs and increase profits.

This is what WTO boss, Renato Ruggerio has to say about the FSIA:

Nations representing over 95% of the trade in banking, insurance, securities and financial information have brought financial services into the realm of international rules. It is through these international rules, agreed by all our members, that businesses can best gain the certainty needed to plan their future international activities.

The impact of this comment in Australia's banking industry can be seen through Australia being party to the WTO's FSIA. Australia's four major banks have eliminated 30,000 full-time jobs since 1991, and are expected to eliminate a further 60,000 by 2005.

With this agreement, the WTO has completed a remarkable year. In 1997, our members agreed on an historic global pact on telecommunications encompassing more than 95% of the global telecommunications market; they agreed to remove all tariffs on information technology products, one of the fastest growing sectors of the global economy; and they agreed, through the High Level Meeting of Least Developed Countries, on a path which will give important impetus to the integration of the world's poorest lands into the multilateral trading system....

The above comment by Ruggerio reveals the real issue driving the privatisation of Telstra – not because it is good for Australia, but because it has been demanded by the new world order at the WTO. Ruggerio continues:

These four events underline the commitment of our member states, both developing and developed, to the process of trade liberalization and globalisation. At a time when many of our citizens feel uncertain about this fast changing world, this commitment provides the foundation for our collective welfare.

We will not rest with these achievements, but will continue to build on them. The commemoration next year of the 50th anniversary of the multilateral trading system provides us all with the opportunity to reflect on the great contribution this system has made to peace and prosperity and to chart our future course in an ever more integrated world.

Can there be any question over who or what is driving major policy issues in Australia? It is not our government, it is big business' WTO.

On December 27, 1997, it was reported that the financial services industry had reduced employment by more than 10 per cent over the past 5 years, despite the sector's burgeoning growth – this is directly related to foreign-control and the FSIA. The finance sector has cut its workforce by over 16% since 1991. The insurance workforce had been cut by over 35% in this period, despite the managed funds industry's 'spectacular growth'. On January 21, 1998, it was announced that National Mutual and MLC would merge, targeting cost reductions of $200 million a year over 3 years by *'removing overlapping functions and through staff cuts'*.

Right now in Australia the four major banks are embarking on a co-ordinated campaign to further reduce the services provided to ordinary Australians. The major beneficiaries will be the overseas shareholders. The co-ordinated assault by the big foreign controlled banks is on what is called *"The Four Pillars Policy"* which is enacted in legislation and has the primary aim of ensuring that Australia's four major banks, the Commonwealth Bank, National Australia Bank, ANZ and Westpac cannot merge – guaranteeing healthy competition.

Unsurprisingly, Michael Kroger, the Liberal powerbroker was *"contracted"* in November 1998 by the National Australia Bank to lobby the Coalition government to help remove the *"Four Pillars Policy"*. NAB's Don Argus told the media days after Kroger's appointment that he was *"extremely confident"* that this goal would now be achieved.

The FSIA

Kroger's efforts have resulted in the formation of a special governmental *"financial services ministry"* to investigate the "Four Pillars policy".

If the policy is removed from legislation our four big banks will become just two at a cost of tens of thousands of Australian jobs and the closure of hundreds of bank branches.

What ever has happened to King O'Malley MHR's dream of financial independence?

The issues:

The four major banks have eliminated 30,000 full-time jobs since 1991, and are expected to eliminate a further 60,000 by 2005. Bank branch closures amounted to 386 – or more than one a day in 1997 with the loss of services mainly affecting the bush.

When the current four pillars policy relating to Australian banks is removed expect National Australia Bank to merge with Westpac. (It is expected that NAB will change its name to reflect a more *"Asian"* market. After all NAB recently threatened to move its head office off-shore to Asia.)

Prime Minister John Howard has publicly said that *this will never happen.* Unless we stop it, it will. The timing is a mere formality now with Liberal powerbroker and merchant banker Michael Kroger earning a healthy retainer and success fee for his work in securing the dismantling of this government policy. When this occurs tens of thousands of jobs in the banking sector will be lost and the loss of proper banking services to a greater proportion of the Australian population will follow.

Expect bank fees to rise dramatically as *"competition"* becomes less of an issue.

Banks will gravitate more and more towards supporting the big business sector while those least able to afford it will find the costs of using the bank's diminishing facilities becoming more and more exorbitant.

With Australia's foreign debt reaching astronomical proportions following our entry into the *"globalised world"*[13] and our banks now being controlled by foreigners we are now at the financial mercy of Wall Street thanks to our career politicians.

[13] From just Au$20 billion in 1983 to over Au$230 billion today

The FSIA

What the major parties think about this issue:

Consider the impassioned claims by both the Coalition and the Labor Party to be about creating "jobs". Now consider the impact of their actions in being party to this one international agreement.

The Labor Party bought Australia into the FSIA. There was no kicking or screaming because the mainstream Australian population had no idea that it was taking place or what the long-term ramifications would be. Bob McMullan's comment in 1995 that *"The financial services agreement will directly benefit Australian banks, insurance companies and securities traders."* is spot on. While these foreign-owned financial industries have flourished under the FSIA hundreds of thousands of Australians have been detrimentally affected by the agreement.

Traditionally the Labor Party has been the voice of the people but this facade is becoming more and more transparent. Their role in signing Australia into globalist treaties that facilitate the greed-based desires of overseas big business to the detriment of the standard of living of the people they represent is only now being exposed.

The Coalition, traditionally closely aligned to big business, has played an active and compliant role in allowing the WTO to secure further compromises for the global banking industry.

When Costello signed the amendments to the FSIA in December 1997 he opened up the floodgates allowing Wall Street to acquire the small state based banks as well. The amendments include the following statement:

Removes an entry relating to the reservations by State and Territory governments of the right to prohibit foreign control of State-owned or controlled banks.

Not surprisingly there has been a recent co-ordinated effort to sell off state owned banks with little or no opportunity for discussion being afforded to the stakeholders – the people living in that state. The most recent example is the sale of the Suncorp-Metway bank in Queensland under the newly formed Labor government.

The Queensland Labor Government had, in the lead-up to the election just a few months before, promised to halt the proposed privatisation which had been flagged by the Coalition government.

How the media have reported on this issue:

The FSIA has gone unreported in the mainstream media.

When major events happen in the banking industry – such as the closing of key bank branches – the cause is never exposed. The mainstream media would have Australians believe that the closing of bank branches and the loss of employment by large numbers of bank staff is a natural progression for a more efficient industry.

The truth is far removed – the fruits of the FSIA represent a classic case study of economic rationalism in action.

The outcome:

Unfortunately it is already too late for our current Australian banks. They have become little more than foreign owned assets... the ownership of our banking industry is now effectively in the hands of the money men in Wall Street.

In the long term, if Australia is to prosper and aspire to reach its full potential, we must establish a publicly owned bank to finance our growth.

On-line research on the FSIA:
http://www.gwb.com.au/gwb/news/mai/fsamain.html

Chapter 3
Economic Rationalism

ABC Background Briefing (7th July 1998): *Economic Rationalism means untold wealth for a very few and poverty for a large number of people. Business executives get obscene salaries while workers get sacked. If labour has no role, democracy has no future.*

Background:

Economic rationalism is one of the primary business philosophies underwriting *"globalisation"*. It is an economic policy, an approach to economic decision making.

This philosophy removes the traditional social responsibility of maintaining the community's standards of living out of the equation. In its place it favours larger profits for and financial returns to, largely, foreign investors. Once this baseline has been accepted social impacts become irrelevant to the decision making process. Today the social conscience image presented by multinationals in their advertising is nothing more than a facade.

As Karl Polanyi[14] says, *"Market economy implies a self-regulating system of markets; in slightly more technical terms, it is an economy directed by market prices and nothing but market prices."*

Polanyi argues that such an idea of an economy is quite extraordinary, *"previously to our time no economy has ever existed that, even in principle, was controlled by markets"*. Instead, in most of human history, *"economic action has been subordinated to and embedded within social relationships"*. The economy served society rather than what happens in a market economy – *"where the roles are reversed and society serves the economy"*.

Polanyi (pg 73) predicted what is happening to our society all those years ago, *To allow the market mechanism to be the sole director of the fate of human beings and their natural environment ... would result in the demolition of society. For the alleged commodity "labour power" cannot be shoved about, used indiscriminately, or even left unused, without affecting also the human individual who happens to be the bearer of this peculiar commodity... Nature*

[14] Polanyi: *The Great Transformation* - pg 43 - was first published in 1944. His book is one of the great texts in economic sociology/ political economy.

would be reduced to its elements, neighborhoods and landscapes defiled, rivers polluted, military safety jeopardized, the power to produce food and raw materials destroyed.

An example of this duplicity can be clearly demonstrated when you consider the chasm between the public profile of a good *"corporate"* citizen and the real hard business-like approach of that famous multinational fast food enterprise McDonalds.

A growing number of people refer to employment under *"economic rationalism"* as McJobs because most work at McDonalds offers no future at very low wages[15].

In a three year defamation case brought by McDonalds against two activists the multinational did not appeal the damning ruling against them by Judge Justice Bell in March 1999 agreeing that he was *"correct in his conclusions"*. These conclusions included the statement that *"various of McDonald's advertisements 'exploit children with their advertising strategy', and 'pay low wages, helping to depress wages in the catering trade'"*.

In Australia McDonalds promoted its service of employing school children as *"training teenagers basic business skills"*. They do this while earning slave-labour youth wages and keeping older people out of work (because of minimum wages payable under the award system). In reality students at McDonalds were learning little more than how to turn a big-Mc, smile or heat up some fries. Their employment (or training) normally ceasing when the students no longer attracted the youth wage.

When the Coalition government warned that they would remove the federal awards *(allowing the standard of living of Australia's working class poor to drop even further)* McDonalds immediately warned that the tens of thousands of students in their employ would lose their jobs. The more experienced and older workers would now be able to be employed by the fast food giant at the same low wages. The *"training"* aspect McDonalds promoted in its *"good citizen"* profile was, in reality, a time based financial burden for the company – inexperienced student labour was dispensable. It was now much cheaper to employ older staff for a longer period of time reducing the need for this training element. The facade of *"training teenagers basic business skills"* was removed as economic rationalism came into play.

---

[15] http://www.gwb.com.au/gwb/news/multi/mclibel.htm

Economic Rationalism

The Coalition's proposed removal of the youth awards is a victory for economic rationalism. It is a tragedy for Australians when you consider that an estimated 5.5 million or 33% of our population are already officially living below the poverty line[16].

McDonalds are not alone in the contrasting "good citizen" image presented through advertising and the business reality that is pursued through economic rationalism. Consider Kelloggs, Coles Myer and Nike shoes to name but a few. The Australian media will never question the multinationals about this and other issues because companies like Kelloggs, Coles and McDonalds are major advertisers worth millions of dollars in revenue.

The basis of economic rationalism is the supporting of the *"free market"* or, in other words, making business more competitive in the new *"globalised"* world where all salaries are linked to the level playing field – the lowest common denominator – the cheapest salaries in the world. We are seeing traditional standard of living in Australia slide down the scale towards those being experienced in Vietnam and Indonesia.

Graham Strachan sums up economic rationalism in this way:

In his book "The Death of Economics"(1994), Paul Ormerod describes the appropriation of the word 'rational' to economic rationalism as 'a propaganda coup of the highest order'. It carries the implication that any criticisms of it, or any alternatives put forward, are by definition 'irrational', and hence not worthy of serious consideration[17].

The 'rational' in economic rationalism comes from philosophy where it means 'guided by reason as opposed to emotions'. Now the term 'emotions' covers a wide field, and includes things like 'consideration for people', or 'sympathy for the plight of human beings', ethical considerations. These things have to be excluded from the economic equation as a matter of policy.

From philosophy the term was applied to the rising 'scientific management' in the late nineteenth century. Scientific management (sometimes called Taylorism after its originator, Frederick Winslow Taylor)[18] *involved the breaking down of jobs into a series*

---

[16] The figures come from a Melbourne University report which was launched by Sir William Deane in March 1998.

[17] Paul Ormerod, "The Death of Economics" (1994) p.111-2.

[18] Harry Braverman, "Labor and Monopoly Capital"(1974), Chapter 4, esp. p.91.

of steps which could be performed by a number of different operatives doing repetitive tasks. This de-skilled and dehumanised the work, and it was known as the 'rationalisation' of work: the organisation of work without regard for the people who did it. People became 'human resources', just another aspect of the production process like raw materials and packaging. To the economic rationalist, people have no other function on earth than as adjuncts to the economic system.

In short 'rational' means without regard for humans, and economic rationalism is the policy that in the making of economic decisions, their effect on people, or the community at large, is not a 'rational' consideration. Now if you think this is an exaggeration, consider this: the Hilmer Report[19]*, an influential document in the implementation of economic rationalism in Australia states, at p.99: '....in determining questions of public benefit, primary emphasis should be placed on economic efficiency considerations'. So if you've been wondering why governments no longer seem to care about the hardship caused by present economic policies on the people of the world, that's why. If you've been wondering why the word 'rationalise' invariable means 'downsizing' a company and the shedding of labour, that's why.*

You might also be wondering what's 'rational' (in the sense of 'sane, sensible, not foolish, absurd, or extreme'), about an economic policy for human beings which specifically excludes its effect on human beings from the economic equation. The answer is, there is nothing rational about it at all. Economic rationalism is about as 'irrational' as it gets. Put bluntly, it involves the insatiable pursuit of profit, and to hell with the human race and its environment.

Economic rationalism is practised by all big businesses today. One reads of tens of thousands of jobs becoming obsolete when two major companies merge or a new chief executive officer takes over at the helm.

A classic example is Telstra, once a business fully owned by the people of Australia, which became the target of bureaucratic economic rationalism. This began when an American, Frank

---

[19] The Hilmer Report: National Competition Policy' (1993) promised lower prices, improved consumer choice, higher economic growth and 'increased employment opportunities for the economy as a whole' [Hilmer Report, p.1].

Blount, was *employed by the people of Australia* to prepare the country's most valuable public asset for privatisation. The infamous Hilmer report and the WTO's agreement on telecommunications paved the way for by-passing the voter once again.

WTO chief Ruggerio said:

With this agreement, the WTO has completed a remarkable year. In 1997, our members agreed on an historic global pact on telecommunications encompassing more than 95% of the global telecommunications market; they agreed to remove all tariffs on information technology products, one of the fastest growing sectors of the global economy; and they agreed, through the High Level Meeting of Least Developed Countries, on a path which will give important impetus to the integration of the world's poorest lands into the multilateral trading system....

Telstra's public shareholders, the Australian people, were never consulted by the bureaucrats about the plans that the WTO had in store for the company through privatisation. Compliant Coalition and Labor governments both played their part in allowing economic rationalism to flourish as tens of thousands of Telstra workers were retrenched as the company was *"rationalised"* to make it more *"profitable"*.

Another example of economic rationalism is the manner in which the Australian banks, following the signing of the WTO's FSIA, retrenched tens of thousands of full time staff. This was great for the bottom line of the foreign banks who took large stakes in the once Australian-owned banks. It was a social calamity for tens of thousands of Australians employed in this industry.

> *Two Mexican local authorities are being sued under Nafta (North American Free Trade Area, a mini-MAI) clauses by United States companies because they were prevented from establishing toxic waste dumps in the jurisdiction of these authorities.*
>
> David Rowan, Guardian Weekly (UK, international), 22 Feb 98

Economic Rationalism

The issues:

Perhaps the most dramatic example of the negative effects of *"economic rationalism"* is the Australian banking industry. Just a few years ago small bank branches were the lifeblood of rural communities. Today many small towns are dying because of a decision made by the bank's board to increase profits with no consideration of the social impact.

Branches are clinically and coldly assessed based on profitability – or the lack of it. A line in the spread sheet determines the fate of those depending on the bank's services.

At this profit-driven cut-off point the decision is made to close bank branches without any consideration for the community effected by the decision.

Tens of thousands of jobs have been lost by ex-bank staff who have fallen victim to decisions made on this basis. When the National Australia Bank's managing director, Don Argus, asked about the impact that his decision to close bank branches was having on his staff he replied that *"that's an emotional issue"*.... discounting the relevance of the question on his bank's decision.

The removal of trade barriers has allowed many of our largely foreign owned economic rationalist based businesses to be moved off-shore. The Australian worker is the loser as he or she cannot compete on the *"level playing field"* in countries like Vietnam where staff doing the same work get paid a fraction of the wage.

The Sydney Morning Herald (October 20, 1997) reported that in the 12 years 1985-1997 *(the era of economic rationalism)* 3.3 million Australian workers had been retrenched and had to find replacement jobs, in what it described as a *'massive downsizing of the nation's labour-force'*. Now of a total of only 8.4 million available jobs, *only 6.3 million are full time*, the rest (26%) are casual or part-time, and that proportion is increasing. Net growth in full-time employment in the 1990s has been zero, due to job destruction by (now foreign-owned) big business.

What the major parties think about this issue:

There is clear evidence that the major parties, and in particular, the Coalition are party to economic rationalism.

The move by Industrial Relations Minister Peter Reith in recent months to remove the minimum award rates which protect the most disadvantaged in our community smacks of this modern malaise.

Economic Rationalism

This move followed the dismantling of the Commonwealth Employment Service (CES) as well as job shedding in other government departments. The CES was aimed at providing a government controlled avenue for the unemployed to gain employment. It has now been replaced by a number of privately owned business contractors who are contracted to fulfil this service through Centrelink – with each successful placement, depending on the length of time the person has been unemployed, resulting in a payment from the government.

When the CES was dismantled some 4,000 employees were retrenched.

Centrelink has been a spectacular failure. What it has achieved, however, is even stricter guidelines for people seeking social welfare support.

These are the people who the Coalition will be pushing into jobs without award wage protection – the teenagers making pocket money being replaced by the older worker trying to live on the same wage while working long hours at McDonalds. The bottom-line for the Coalition is the all important and rubbery *"unemployment"* figure – reduce it at any cost to the standards of living in the country. This begs the question just who does our elected government represent?

Perhaps the answer is so easy to uncover when you understand that all major electoral funding to the Labor and Coalition parties at election time is provided by big business.

The result of the Coalition's economic rationalist actions in the area of social support services has been growing queues reported at all branches of privately run community service organisations providing free food to the poor.

Just a few years ago it would have been inconceivable to consider the need for a service like this in Australia – the lucky country.

The Labor Party have, through their involvement in international agreements like the FSIA, been willing partners in the move towards economic rationalism. Their partners, the Australian Council of Trade Unions (ACTU) *(which all Labor's Federal MPs are members of)* have been playing politics when they claim that they have instigated an investigation into awards and employment. The investigation through the International Labour Organisation (ILO) resulted in this international body *"Blowing the Whistle"* on Australia's new labour laws – but nothing has changed.

How the media have reported on this issue:

The media have remained distant from one of the underlying issues behind the growing number of employed and poverty stricken people in Australia.

When reporting on the social impact aspect of economic rationalism the social failings of this economic philosophy are rarely, if ever, questioned. The great divide in objective reporting on the growing poverty in Australia is the lack of questioning what is behind it happening.

Is there a solution:

There is a simple solution - make blatant acts of economic rationalism – such as those being thrust upon the population by the banks come at considerable financial cost. Collateral damage to communities through profit-based closures should be financially compensated where they cannot be prevented. Furthermore, laws should be enacted giving priority to upholding social and community standards in Australia.

As an example, banks should not be allowed to close a branch in a small community if the people there will be adversely effected by the loss of this critical financial backbone.

Where staff are retrenched, not because of business failure but because of economic rationalism principles, the business shown to be embarking on this strategy should be responsible for providing substantial financial long-term support to those who are displaced until they once again gain employment.

On-line research on economic rationalism: http://www.gwb.com.au/gwb/news/economic

Chapter 4
Sell-Off Of The farm

The *"new world order"* has been in development for decades, and did not originate with President George Bush in 1990. The *"old world order"* is one based on independent nation-states. The *"new world order"* involves the elimination of the sovereignty and independence of nation-states and some form of world government. This means the end of Australia, its constitution, judicial system etc.

Most of the new world order proposals involve the conversion of Australia to part of a world government, complete with a world army, a world parliament, a World Court, global taxation, and numerous other agencies to control every aspect of human life (education, nutrition, health care, population, immigration, communications, transportation, commerce, agriculture, finance, the environment, etc.).

The various notions of the *"new world order"* differ as to details and scale, but agree on the basic principle and substance. The power brokers will be the multinationals and their directors.

Background:

Australia is recognised as one of the wealthiest countries in the world, with estimated mineral resources alone being worth close to Au$1 million per capita. One would think that as an *"independent"* country that wealth would reflect on the standard of living of the community that resides there.

Although this could have and should be the case, the political shenanigans of the major parties has allowed many of these public and resource based assets to fall into foreign hands.

Mineral resources:

Most mines of any consequence today are controlled or fully owned by foreign based mining giants like Rio Tinto. The irony behind this sell-off is no better demonstrated than in the conflicting manner in which proposed mining developments in areas claimed under native title are treated. The complication of *"political correctness"* has a positive side after all!

Take the Century Zinc mine in northern Queensland as an example. This billion dollar development, controlled by foreign interests, was delayed for several years while the people, not the politicians, negotiated terms for the prospective developers. This included a substantial monetary payout equalling many millions of dollars to the small Aboriginal communities who had native title rights over the effected land.

No such negotiation or discussion is allowed where lands fall outside native title claims. The foreign multinationals simply bid for the asset with unlimited access to funding or, like in the case of Chase Manhattan Nominees, take a large controlling equity in the company managing the mining of the Australian asset.

The manner in which our mineral wealth is being exploited is just one example of what is happening behind the scenes to traditional Australian icons of value.

Household names like Vegemite, Arnotts Biscuits, Aeroplane Jelly, Kambrook, the Commonwealth Bank, Kraft, Pauls Icecream and Qantas – to name but a few are now effectively owned and controlled by boardrooms in foreign lands.

In most cases these Australian assets, once taken over by a foreign business, follow a natural progression towards economic rationalism with the coup-de-grace coming when the manufacturing aspect is shut down and moved into an Asian country where employees earn as little as US$39 per month[20].

The rural sector:

Land values in the rural sector have been decimated in Australia – not only by the removal of tariffs, but also by the uncertainty of native title claims on Australian owned pastoral leases. The fall in values has made the ownership of large tracts of Australia, a politically stable country, by foreign owners very attractive.

While the government of Japan is highly protective over land ownership by foreigners, the Australian government has seen fit to make this an easy option for anybody who flashes a few million dollars in front of the eyes of the well-connected.

A classic example is that of the massive property in the Northern Territory known as Tipperary.

Tipperary is Australia's tenth largest land holding (1.9 million hectares). It includes eight properties in the Northern Territory. The company began as a joint venture between the Australian property developer Warren Anderson and Indonesian-based Bakire and

---

[20] This is the case in Vietnam.

Brothers. Bakire bought out Mr Anderson[21] in 1994 and today runs 65,000 Brahman cattle on the Tipperary lease.

Indonesia's cattle fattening industry is based in Lampung with the company, PT Tipperary Indonesia, running these fattening yards in central Lampung. PT Tipperary is owned by the Bakire family. Cattle for fattening are shipped directly to Lampung from the Northern Territory.

The double whammy for the Australian rural industry is that while Bakire has a monopoly over the supply of meat to Indonesia he uses Australia's own resources to exploit this home advantage over potential Australian beef suppliers. The cattle are shipped, live, to Indonesia resulting in the loss of any financial benefit, whatsoever, to Australia. No abattoirs, no employment, no value-added exports... no expose about the un-Australian developments in the media.

The National Farmers Federation (NFF) belies its aim as the custodian protecting the interests of the rural sector. Today the NFF largely represent the interests of big business in the rural sector.

In 1986 the NFF launched a 'fighting fund' allegedly to save the family farm, and collected about $15 million from farmers. The money was never used for the stated purpose, but was put into a trust fund where it apparently remains to this day. Small family farm businesses were told they had to become *'more competitive'*, they had to *'get big or get out'*.

Farmers followed the advice of the NFF and borrowed money to get big, then they went broke trying to pay the interest. Thousands have simply walked off the family farm destitute. 60% of the Australian-owned farming sector has been wiped out. In the 1960s there were 300,000 farms, now there are around 100,000.

At the end of 1997 the remaining farmers were leaving the land at the rate of 35 per week according to Primary Industry Minister John Anderson[22]. Those who remain are now heavily in debt. In mid-1996 they owed $18 billion to banks, an average of $133,000 per farm. Today (1999) this figure has blown out to $260,000 with about 20% of remaining farmers in *"severe financial distress"*.[23]

---

[21] It was at about this time that Warren Anderson joined Paul Keating on a trip to Indonesia when Keating was trying to sell his equity in the debt-laden piggery.

[22] On ABC.TV's "First Wednesday" programme in August, 1997

[23] Australian Bureau of Statistics

Sell-Off Of The Farm

In response to the plight of the Australian farmer the Australian government put up a $500 million *'rural assistance'* package to help farmers leave the land. The privately-owned Australian 'family' farm is scheduled for destruction through this government policy. Foreign multinationals are set to own and control Australia's farming sector. That's *'globalisation'*.

Privatisation:

In the major cities privatisation of public utilities is now conducted without question, and without any discussion with the people in the street. The privatisation of public utilities is nothing more than a fire-sale allegedly aimed at trying to recoup some of the massive debt that we now face as Australians. Tragically the foreign buyers of these public utilities are allowed to borrow money to pay for them. The result is that the billions of dollars that they borrow is simply lumped onto this country's foreign debt. The result is the transfer of that portion of the foreign debt from the public to the private sector while the country's balance sheet and its perilously high paper debt remains unchanged.

The Hilmer Report, the blue-print behind privatisation, states *that "The ownership of a business is not of itself a matter of direct concern from a competition policy perspective"*. In other words privatising a government-owned corporation or public utility will not in itself increase competition. Not only that, but it is likely to be detrimental to the public interest. Privatisation converts a goal *of 'service to the public'* into a goal of *'profit regardless of the public'*, which will almost guarantee there will be price rises, as there always are in practice. So privatisation is of no benefit to the public.

Perhaps the most dramatic example of the privatisation of a single public entity (after the Commonwealth Bank) is the proposed sale of the whole of Telstra. When Australia's largest public entity was handed over to an American, Frank Blount, to control the alarm bells should have rung.

They didn't.

Jobs were shed, the industry was redesigned to open it up to the WTO's blue-print of foreign competition and then the inevitable was announced by the Coalition government. Telstra was to be privatised – and it is important to note that, despite the rhetoric, the Labor party would have followed exactly the same route if they had been in government. *After all Labor privatised the now foreign controlled Commonwealth Bank of Australia and Qantas without question.*

Graham Strachan sums up privatisation thus,

The purpose of 'privatisation' is to transfer ownership and control of all publicly-owned assets, including essential services, out of the ownership and control of national governments into the hands of internationalists. There is to be no Australian-owned national economy, and the fraudulent policy of 'privatisation' is one of the ways the Australian government can assist the engineers of 'globalisation' to achieve that goal. Again the language of 'free market economics' is used to conceal the real nature of the 'globalisation' process.

Privatisation is just an end product of another tool that impacts dramatically on the local industry. The impact of the removal of tariff protection on Australian industries, most recently the pig and citrus fruit industries, is now spelling the death knell of many local small businesses.

The citrus or fresh orange juice industry is effectively dead in the district of Sunraysia today with massive quantities of low cost orange juice being imported without trade tariffs from Brazil - a country where employees earn a fraction of the wages of Australian labourers. The major retailers like Woolworths and Coles-Myer, with their massive buying power have by-passed local producers because the cost per litre is marginally cheaper – despite shipping costs. No consideration is given to the effected local industry or the impact that such a decision has on our foreign debt.

This is a direct result of the *"globalisation"* that Alexander Downer would have us believe is employment generating.

The Queensland pig industry was, until the mid-1990s a profitable business. *(You have to ask no other authority than ex-Prime Minister Paul Keating who's financial dabblings in this industry resulted in many unanswered questions – including massive unpaid loans being absorbed by the Commonwealth Bank).*

The issues:

The major issue here is the re-distribution of wealth. Australian assets are being sold to foreign companies. Land and resources are now largely in the hands of foreign based entities.

Even our traditional public assets such as electricity and water are being sold to unknown multinationals.

Sell-Off Of The Farm

Australia is fast becoming the equivalent of a home in which every utility, every piece of furniture, every book and even the wallpaper is on lease from a third party. Australians no longer own Australia but are indebted to the tune of hundreds of billions of dollars to the external forces of the globalisation regime.

The sell-off of the farm has now gone so far that many doubt that we can recover any sense of sovereignty in key areas such as financial independence in our local banking industry.

Today an estimated 80% of day-to-day business in Australia is controlled by businesses off-shore.

The only major asset still in Australian hands today is home ownership. While our resources have been sold off at bargain basement prices to foreigners the privilege of home ownership itself is a Clayton's Curse. Most home buyers today are beholden to the foreign owned banks with this traditional investment for the future, in most cases, becoming an impediment to asset growth as fewer and fewer Australians can afford to enjoy home ownership.

What the major parties think about this issue:

Both the Labor and the Coalition parties have been active participants in the sell-off of Australia to multinationals.

Consider the words of Kim Beazley mirrored by Alexander Downer along the lines that *"globalisation is good for Australia"*.

How the media have reported on this issue:

The media have skirted around the sale of Australian assets to foreign multinationals. No concerns have been raised, no questions asked. It is accepted as *"inevitable"*.

In November 1998 the *Courier-Mail* made a stunning remark the day after the publicly owned Suncorp/Metway Bank was floated for Au$1.5 billion. The remark was that the share price had jumped 40% *on the day of the float*. The Murdoch press (who's top five shareholders include Chase Manhattan Nominees - one of the major beneficiaries of the float) said that the rise was a *"windfall"* for the small Queensland mum and dad voters. These mum and dad voters were restricted to just 300 shares each because of over-subscription with 40% of the sale going to *"institutional"* investors like the Bank of Hawaii.

In reality this asset owned by these Queenslanders was *undervalued by 40% or about Au$600 million...* enough funding to build a number of schools and to remove all hospital waiting lists for years. The profit went into the hands of those who acquired the shares on the day the public entity was floated – the big losers were the people of Queensland.

The media totally overlooked the reality of this loss to the people of Queensland brought about by this privatisation of a public asset.

Is there a solution:

Public assets must remain in public hands. They are the lifeblood to the maintenance of the standard of living that Australians have come to enjoy.

Under public control the government will be forced to ensure that a balance in meeting the needs of the community will be maintained.

The control of Australian resources must stay in Australian hands.

The simple strategy that *"foreign investment is good, foreign ownership is bad"* should be the bottom-line in all issues relating to ownership of Australian assets.

Assets now controlled by foreign entities must be taxed at a fair and equitable rate. This should include a financial loading based on the ability of these businesses to strip core assets out of the ground with no proportional benefit to the Australian people.

Chapter 5
The Privatisation Of Telstra

> *The Final Act of the Uruguay Round, marking the conclusion of the most ambitious trade negotiation of our century, will give birth - in Morocco - to the WTO, the third pillar of the New World Order, along with the United Nations and the International Monetary Fund.*
>
> Part of a full-page advertisement by the government of Morocco in the New York Times (April 1994)

Background:

There is no clearer example of the current hijacking of the Australian economy by overseas forces than the current fracas over the sale of Telstra.

The Coalition sold 33% of Telstra, a publicly owned asset, in 1997 on the instruction of the WTO. Much was made in the media of the *"public's ability to acquire shares"* in an asset that they already owned. The sale followed the Hilmer report recommendations of deregulation as covered in the previous chapter. It also followed an investigation of the *"monopolistic"* Telstra by the Australian Competition and Consumer Commission (ACCC) *(which, despite its name, is no friend of the Australian public)* in 1995. The end result was the Telstra Bill of 1996.

It was Alan Asher, the deputy at the ACCC, and earlier one of Australia's delegates to the UN on transnational corporations, who said on ABC Radio in November 1997 when defending the MAI,

"I've for a long time had difficulty in believing that there is such a thing as national sovereignty any more. Now whether that's a good thing or not is something that's up to individuals. But if you look at the huge proportion of our lives, that is inherently trans-border, whether it's culture, the economy, the environment, law enforcement, even the weather, even the smoke in Asia knows no national boundaries.

"And so for people who want to cling to a notion of national sovereignty that's built along lines of geography on a map, it's my perception that that's something that is just no longer a tenable option. And if that's the case, then it's not of much help trying to isolate oneself from the world, and it seems to me that maybe that's part of the problems of the Malaysian financial system, where

they've tried to isolate themselves from pressures that you simply can't resist any longer."

In other words, in the view of the powerful ACCC deputy, Australia should just give up trying to be a sovereign nation and sell-up the entire farm. That is exactly what the ACCC seems to be trying to achieve through approving the sale of Telstra and deregulation in the telecommunications area.

This process started with the large scale rationalisation of Telstra taking place shortly before the initial sale. This followed the appointment of an American economic rationalist, Frank Blount, as chief executive officer. Tens of thousands of Telstra jobs have since been lost *"in the interests of the company's competitiveness"*. In reality the Telstra cow was being prepared for sale to multinationals waiting in the wings.

The financial stupidity of the sale of this publicly owned asset at this time can best be compared to the assumption that Bill Gates should sell his share of Microsoft shortly after releasing the Windows software program to the world. No businessman in his right mind would do such a thing - in Gates' case, the business was entering an exciting new growth phase.

Since Windows was released in the early 1990s the value of Microsoft has exploded and, no, Gates did not sell his share of the company – as a result he is the wealthiest man in the world today.

Telstra is at the forefront of the new communications age.

If you consider the Microsoft example one thing is for sure, the profitability of our still, largely publicly owned telecommunications giant, will explode because of new technologies like the Internet. Since the sale of one third of Telstra went ahead the value of the shares has risen by 180% and profits being made by the giant have exploded from just Au$1 billion a year in 1995 to a figure approaching Au$4 billion a year in 1999.

So why is the Coalition government hell-bent on selling Telstra?

Because the WTO is demanding that it does and compliant Australian bureaucrats, advising the politicians, are acting in accordance with the organisation's demands that their laws supersede Australia's community interests.

Currently one third of Telstra's profits are taxed fairly (unlike the standard tax avoidance routines practised by the multinationals), and the profits returned to government revenue. That is over Au$3 billion annual return on the Australian public's asset – shareholders whose taxes and investments have allowed it to become what it has.

The Privatisation Of Telstra

The Coalition's public face for the push on the sale of Telstra is based on a 'commitment' *that foreign ownership will be restricted to just 35%.* The ALP when making the decision to sell off the Commonwealth Bank of Australia – stated that the ownership of the bank would *never be allowed* leave Australian shores. Wrong – it is – thanks to the Coalition's amendment to the FSIA!

Since making this commitment Communications Minister Senator Alston has ducked the question of foreign ownership of Telstra by asking which government would want to change the guidelines currently being proposed by the Coalition.

In the weeks leading up to the vote in the Senate for the sale of Telstra in the Senate Rod Kemp, the Assistant Treasurer, wrote in the Weekend Australian (21/3/98):

I note that a number of contributors to the Letters to the Editor have claimed that the proposed Multilateral Agreement on Investment (MAI) would prohibit the Government placing restrictions on foreign ownership of Telstra.

This is not the case. Under the MAI being negotiated all countries, including Australia, will be able to lodge exceptions, including one covering floats of public corporations.

This would ensure that the Government reserves the right to undertake such floats on the basis that it determines.

Despite the many claims to the contrary, Australia's exceptions to the proposed treaty would remain in place as long as the Government so determines.

The Government would not agree to the MAI if it did not permit exceptions or if it required that exceptions must be repealed after a particular period of time.

Indeed, the government will not agree to this, or any other treaty, unless it is demonstrably in Australia's national interest.

Protecting our national interest involves ensuring that any agreement on the MAI does not override or weaken our current domestic policies, whilst ensuring that the treaty delivers benefits to Australians and Australian investors.

The duplicity of Kemp's words highlighted in his letter above can be revealed by the fact that the Coalition government had been negotiating the MAI on this basis until the Joint Standing Committee on Treaties was formed just weeks before (see chapter one on globalisation and the MAI).

The proposed sale of Telstra in its entirety in 1998, coupled with the hidden imposition of the MAI would soon have resulted in the loss of an asset which was and is set to explode in value. The timing was perfect until the whistle was blown on the multinationals' MAI strategy and just one vote in the Senate stopped the sale of Telstra from proceeding after One Nation's impact started being felt in the bush. It all come down to one simple fact – that politicians elected to represent the Australian people are clearly dancing to someone else's tune.

That one vote in the Senate was ex-Labor MP Senator Mal Colston, who had a habit of voting with the Coalition, the proponents of the sale of Telstra, following his falling out with Labor. Colston told the Senate he was worried about the sale's impact on Telstra jobs and services - especially those in rural Queensland. He said that he was also concerned about the standards of telecommunications delivery to the bush - pointing out that, despite promises that they would get better prior to the sale of one third of the communications giant, services to the bush had in fact worsened.

"For us to do otherwise would be to short change our future for short term political gain. On balance I find at this stage I am unable to support the Bill and will thus be voting against it."

Colston joined the Labor Party, Democrats and Greens voting against the sale. Independent Brian Harradine joined the Coalition forcing a stunningly close 34 vote tie and the rejection of the sale.

Harradine had carefully negotiated his support and had, as a result, been guaranteed that a small Telstra office in Tasmania employing less than 20 staff would not be closed down after the sale. As you will see guarantees, even to a Senator, mean nothing.

It is horrifying to think that such an enormous asset could have been sold at that time. Twelve months later its value has appreciated dramatically. All this would have been lost to the Australian people.

In all of this it is important to note the personal involvement of Prime Minister John Howard in the push for the sale of Telstra. Howard flew up to Queensland to see Colston just before the vote – his mission was to get Colston to support the sale.

When Colston talked about the effect on employment following the proposed sale one should consider the impact of the FSIA on the banking industry. The four major banks have eliminated 30,000 full-time jobs since 1991, and are expected to eliminate a further 60,000 by 2005. Entire rural shires like Kilkivan no longer have a single bank. Those worst effected by a sale of Telstra are, no doubt, again those in the rural sector.

Since that vote was taken Independent Brian Harradine has also realised the folly of voting for the sale of any additional part of Telstra. This follows the breaking of the commitment by the telecommunications giant under Blount that it would not close down a small service centre in Tasmania which employed just sixteen people. Telstra went ahead and closed the facility down despite its commitment to Harradine following the initial failed vote. Quite simply, as Harradine pointed out in the Senate in 1999, the Coalition could not be trusted to keep their word and he would no longer support them in the sale of Telstra.

The Coalition then embarked on a highly public last ditch attempt to woo Harradine by publicly promising to change the laws in relation to the Internet and pornography – opening the gate for censorship.

Publicly owned and funded Telstra had earlier financed News Corp's Foxtel Pay television services to the tune of hundreds of millions of dollars. In April 1999 Murdoch started getting impatient over the failed sale demanding that Telstra sell its share in the pay TV operation at a time it was starting to show its first profits.

It is instructive to compare what has happened to the services of the telecommunications industry once the government starts interfering with it.

Before the government sold 33% of Telstra it opened up the telecommunications market to foreign competitors like Optus. This despite the American experience in this industry. In the USA AT&T's monopoly on calls was removed in 1984. The removal of the monopoly resulted in some 1,200 separate operating companies, each of them with different prices, some with universal access, some without, *"offering competition"* to AT&T. They were, in reality, nothing more than fragments on the old AT&T entity. Telephoning in the US today is now so complicated that consumers have to receive a constant stream of material explaining a *'bewildering array of changing rates and services'*. Making a call across the US can result in multiple and complex connections with efficiency being the loser.

Australia is currently protected from a similar chaotic situation arising because Telstra has a monopoly on all local phone lines – something which the new competitors are actively trying to destroy.

The Privatisation Of Telstra

British Telecom was forced to raise the cost of its residential services after it was privatised by the Thatcher government on 1984 and competition was introduced. As a direct result local calls in the UK are, for householders, considerably higher than in Australia. Today British household telephone users are paying more – competition in the telecommunications industry in the UK now being geared towards attracting big business – skewing the promised benefits of *"privatisation"* away from the people who once owned the public utility.

The issues:

The greatest impact of changes through partial privatisation coupled with the new economic rationalism drive in Telstra have already been felt in the bush. The grand hypocrisy is Prime Minister John Howard claiming that only a full sale of Telstra will allow the government to spent a promised Au$90 million on upgrading services for those in rural areas. This is palpable nonsense – as a publicly owned asset earning billions of dollars it should not be entirely profit driven but also concentrate on supporting those Australians in areas where it is not profitable.

This is the line in the sand between social conscience and economic rationalism. Howard is parroting the tune of the economic rationalists. Perhaps he, as Prime Minister does not realise the enormity of his comment...

To sell this asset at any time, let alone when the communications industry is blossoming is madness. Privatisation will see billions of dollars in potential growth being lost.

What the major parties think about this issue:

The Coalition have been trying to push the sale of Telstra using a number of levers to gain the support of key Independents Mal Colston and Brian Harradine in the Senate.

One has got to wonder as to whom is actually pushing their buttons.

Harradine has already publicly stated that the Coalition cannot be trusted following the manner in which Telstra and the government reneged on a simple undertaking.

Labor have got it right, but when one considers how they sold off the Commonwealth Bank of Australia and Qantas and, more recently, the manner in which Beattie sold off Suncorp/Metway, like the Coalition they cannot be trusted.

The Privatisation Of Telstra

This is what Labor says about the sale of Telstra,

Selling Telstra now is like selling off Kalgoorlie before the goldrush.

In the year ending June 1998, Telstra paid a dividend of $1.2 billion to the Commonwealth Government as Telstra's majority shareholder.

This dividend will continue to grow into the future.

Indeed, reflecting the rapidly growing telecommunications market in Australia, and Telstra's continually improving performance, financial commentators expect Telstra's dividend to grow rapidly in the near future.

Respected international merchant bank, Deutsche Morgan Grenfell (DMG), recently observed that:

> *"Like most telecommunications companies, there is little argument about Telstra's capacity to increase returns to shareholders in the future. This is one of the factors underpinning the company's share price performance since listing and is the subject of constant speculation by the market."*
>
> *DMG, Fund Managers' Digest, 27 March 1998*

How the media have reported on this issue:

The mainstream media have never covered the financial stupidity of selling Telstra at this stage.

News Corporation and Telstra's interests in Foxtel combine to provide the basis for a potent cocktail of lies and big business based propagated outcomes with Murdoch being the winner to the expense of all Australians.

Is there a solution:

Yes, do not sell Telstra! Buy back the shares that have been privatised contrary to the wishes of the people and stop the deregulation of this industry.

Chapter 6
Trade Tariffs

"You are surrounded by countries with high tariff policies. Why are you doing this?" Managing Director of Hoechst Australia (Feb '97) commenting on his company's decision to quit the local plastics industry.

Background:

Abraham Lincoln said, *"I don't know much about the tariff. But I know this much. When we buy manufactured goods abroad, we get the goods and the foreigner gets the money. When we buy manufactured goods at home, we get both the goods and the money."*

Sensible words – but the media would have you believe that that is a simplistic notion in the face of the unstoppable globalisation.

The Lima agreement is one of the key foundation stones of globalisation – it is all about the removal of trade tariffs in Australia.

Page 643 of the Lima agreement reads:

Preference should be given by the more industrialised developing countries, as far as possible, to imports of goods produced by the less industrialised countries[24]*. Positive policies are needed to increase intra-regional and interregional trade in manufacturing;*

Read this to mean Australia must remove trade tariffs and import cheaper goods from poorer countries.

Page 645 of the Lima agreement reads:

In the context of international monetary reform, in which the link between financial resources for development purposes and the allocation of special drawing rights is being studied, urgent consideration should be given to the adoption of measures which take account of the particular needs of developing countries. In all phases of decision making for the formulation of a reformed monetary system, full and effective participation of the developing countries in all bodies entrusted with this reform, particularly in the Board of Governors of the International Monetary Fund, in accordance with the existing and evolving rules of such bodies;

[24] Read this as reducing or removing trade tariffs like Australia have.

Trade Tariffs

It is important to realise that Australia was a willing signatory to the Lima agreement under a Labor government in March 1975. It was subsequently supported without question by the Coalition.

The Lima Declaration and Plan of Action called for the redistribution of world industry so that developing countries would have 25% of it by the year 2000. To achieve this, radical changes in traditional concepts and practices were recommended.

Economic growth in poorer countries could no longer be seen as the "trickle down" benefit of growth in rich countries. To close the gap between rich and poor nations the developing countries would have to grow faster than the developed countries. With this end in mind, the Lima Declaration sets out the "main principles of industrialisation" and defines the "means by which the international community as a whole might take broad action to establish a New International Economic Order".

"...the developed countries should assist the developing countries in raising the competitiveness of their production"

In effect the reverse was the hidden agenda with countries like Australia removing their tariff protection – allowing multinationals to tap into cheap labour in Asia replacing existing Australian jobs.

This is enshrined under Section 59 of the Lima agreement Australia is bound to:

"... a progressive elimination or reduction of tariff and non-tariff barriers, and other obstacles of trade... including processed agricultural products"..

Trade tariffs were originally imposed by governments to protect their local industries from *"unfair"* competition in countries where cheap labour, for example, played a major role in the end price of the finished product – and would result in a deterioration of the country's standards of living.

Recently governments in Australia have removed trade tariff barriers – following the script of the Lima agreement. This has resulted in cheaper imports flooding into the country and *"killing-off"* once blossoming Australian industries.

The worst effected is the clothing and textile industry which is, to all intents and purposes, dead in this country. Australian based businesses simply cannot compete with factories in Asia where employees earn just a dollar after working a ten hour day. These Asian factories are little more than slave labour camps with children often making up a percentage of the workers.

Trade Tariffs

Under the drive for globalisation and the *"level playing field"* the end result of removing trade tariffs is the reduction in the standard of living of the population of Australia. It has got to be noted that this detrimental impact only effects the worker and not the multinational company – which is rewarded by increased profits through lower labour costs.

The Lima agreement and subsequent agreements like the Uruguay Round Agreement on GATT (General Agreement on Trade and Tariffs), FSIA and MAI have all had one aim in mind – the globalisation of the world through the dismantling of the sovereignty and financial independence of nations. The MAI and FSIA have been covered in other chapters in this book.

The new owners and operators of trade and economies, like that in Australia, will be an alliance of multinationals which are becoming larger and larger as they merge and form de-facto governments through their sheer financial power[25].

Trade tariffs were one of the biggest safeguards for the sovereignty of countries like Australia. Safeguards that ensured that the country maintained its independence from the financial threats that we face today.

Casualties of the great scam behind removing trade tariffs has now spread to other Australian industries. One of the worst effected is the rural industry. Once a cornerstone of Australia's economy it has become little more than the whipping boy of globalist interests. You have to look no further than the impact of the removal of tariff protection on the pig and citrus fruit industries.

The citrus or fresh orange juice industry is effectively dead in Australia today with massive consignments of low cost orange juice being imported without trade tariffs from Brazil - a country where employees earn a fraction of the wages of Australian labourers[26]. A direct result of the *"globalisation"* that Alexander Downer would have us believe is employment generating.

Who can ever forget the images of orange farmers destroying over 500,000 well-established (up to 40 year-old) orange trees in the Sunraysia district in 1997 after trade tariffs were removed and

---

[25] Over half of the top 100 revenue earners are multinationals – not countries.

[26] This follows the collapse of the Brazilian economy because of the country's inability to fund its foreign debt (consider Australia's position today).

big business like Coles Myer started importing *"cheaper"* juice from Brazil. What happened to the flow-on reduction in orange juice prices to the Australian consumer and what did the Coalition government do when the farmers went to Canberra to protest? The politicians turned their back on all of us. While Brazil has a 40% tariff protection on this industry Australia had none.

Brazilian orange juice is mixed with a small quantity of Australian product, packaged in Australia and then, deceptively, labelled as *"Product of Australia"*.

The Queensland pig industry was, until the mid-1990s, a profitable business to be in.

Import duty levied on Australian exports:

Country	Oranges	Canned Tomatoes	Canned Pears	Pork
United States	$20/tonne	13.6%	16.6%	$18/tonne
European Union	10%	17.4%	19.6-30.9%	2.5-10%
Thailand	60%	30-45%	30%	60%
Taiwan	40%	30%	50%	15%

In March 1999 2UE talk back host Alan Jones said,

"I really don't understand the rules about international trade. Earlier this month we had an International trade Commission in Washington where producers in America were urging high tariff protection to block the entry of lamb into the United States market US sheep producers were saying stick up a tariff wall. Yet we get kicked in the teeth by the WTO for not allowing imports of foreign salmon from Canada and the United States – Canada has been whingeing about it for years but our salmon growers argue correctly that there are 24 diseases in North American salmon while our Tasmanian salmon is disease free.

"We have got the WTO threatening to take the big stick to us and American farmers say we shouldn't be allowed to maintain existing export levels of lamb to America. You see Americans whack a tariff of 132% on peanut butter to protect American peanut farmers. Their sugar quotas are so tough that US sugar prices are about three times the world price. They have got tariffs of between 14 and 32% on most synthetic, woollen and cotton clothing, light trucks attract a tariff of 25%. Coastal and inland shipping in America is restricted to boats registered and built in America. No chance for Australia's fast ferry industry.

Trade Tariffs

"So if US interests are threatened they just adopt protectionist policies that they condemn in other countries. Now we find that Japan are going to stick a massive tariff on any increase to Japan of Australian rice. We are the second largest exporter of rice to Japan.

"But the point is this the Americans and the Japanese don't offer any apology - they just say we have got to do this to protect American and Japanese businesses and jobs but Australia loses on both fronts. We can't get our lamb into America or our increased rice into Japan but we're supposed to open the gate to north American salmon.

"It would be fascinating to know what the theoreticians in Canberra are doing about all this."

The issues:

The removal of trade and tariff protection in this country has destroyed many sound Australian industries. Those most effected are in the small business sector while big business, with its new globalist approach, simply moves its factories off-shore to countries where labour is cheap, or conditions allow it to produce product at a lower cost.

The clothing and textile industry has been the biggest loser with this once large Australian industry now dead and buried with the jobs it once offered now being filled by cheap labour in countries like Vietnam. Australia now imports what it once produced adding to our foreign debt burden.

The end result is increasing unemployment. In the early 1980s unemployment stood at just 1.5% while today *under*employment stands at over 20%. I say underemployment because according to the government's revised guidelines on defining "unemployment" a person is "employed" if he or *she works just one hour a week.* Even on this basis unemployment today stands at close to 10%.

What the major parties think about this issue:

The major parties have been willing partners to the removal of trade and tariffs which have traditionally protected key industries. They continue to do this in a clearly planned approach.

They have both actively supported the Lima agreement philosophy of *"a progressive elimination or reduction of tariff and non-tariff barriers, and other obstacles of trade... including processed agricultural products".*

How the media have reported on this issue:

The media have skirted around the impact that the removal of tariffs has had on employment in this country.

The Murdoch/Packer empires have got the most to gain from globalisation. Their greed-based agenda is reflected in their media empires lack of objective reporting on this issue.

Is there a solution:

There is a simple solution. Trade tariffs have got to be re-introduced in key industries in Australia. Industries that should be immediately targeted with tariff protection are clothing and textiles, the rural sector and general manufacturing industries.

Chapter 7
Deregulation

> *But governments come and governments go. And governments can change their minds. That's why we need a set of rules that will bind governments to levels of behaviour.*
> Steve Canner, US Council for International Business, on Australian radio.

Background:

Deregulation, we are told, will make things *"cheaper"* as the industry becomes more competitive. It is a key underlying requirement for economic rationalists. Unfortunately things do not get cheaper - but the word actually embodies *"unemployment"* and *"inevitable price rises"*. Deregulation is often nothing more than a quick and simple way for big business to force out small business competitors or to break down the pillars supporting a powerful publicly owned asset.

The petroleum industry is an excellent example of the impact of deregulation on small business.

Small petrol station franchises have traditionally been held by small mum and dad businesses. These franchisees signed agreements with petrol companies like BP which allowed them to develop a business supplying petrol to motorists from facilities owned by the petrol company.

Many franchisees had built up excellent businesses and, despite many years of loyal service that they had honoured under these agreements they suddenly found the petrol companies refusing to renew the contracts. The government simply changed the rules under the guise of deregulation. An estimated 10,000 jobs were lost in the industry around Australia as a result.

The official reason for deregulating the petroleum industry was the line spun by Federal treasurer Peter Costello who promised Australians in January 1998 that the deregulation of the petroleum industry would provide a positive result through lower petrol prices at the pump. This never eventuated.

The end-result, in reality, was the emergence of petrol stations at major shopping centres. This further centralised the power and control of the major food chains like Woolworths over their small business competitors. The double whammy came when these major retailers offered *"discount"* petrol to their customers.

These *"discount"* prices are but a passing phase while the smaller petrol distributors are weeded out. Once they have gone the price will rise along the lines of the price of milk in Queensland which demonstrates another little-understood failing of deregulation.

In January 1999 the Queensland State Government deregulated this industry because it promised to make the industry more competitive and lead to lower prices. This was justified under the guidelines of the infamous *"National Competition Policy"*.

The reality could not have been further from the truth. Just three months later on Easter weekend the two prevailing milk distributors, Italian-owned Paul's and major retail chain subsidiary Dairy Farmers announced that there would be a six cent a litre price rise to $1.23 a litre. Weeks earlier, under deregulation, the dairy farmers had been forced to accept a reduction of six cents a lire - getting under 59 cents a litre. They would not be rewarded following the price rise. All of a sudden Australia's dairy industry was, to quote Democrats rural spokesman John Woodley, *"at the crossroads"*.

This led Queensland State Premier Peter Beattie to say after the horse had bolted, *"The Victorian thing may well cost us thousands of jobs (in the dairy industry)"*. What Beattie was talking about was the expected flood of cheap milk from Victoria when its industry is deregulated next year.

Meanwhile Dairy Farmers Queensland manager, John O'Hara explained the price rise thus, *"prices have been kept artificially low by regulation..."*

The end result? Thousands of jobs lost, milk prices rise and the sole beneficiaries are the multinational supermarket chains.

As it was put so succinctly by a wag, *"the cows were not the only ones being milked"*.

Graham Strachan sums up the role of deregulation thus:

To dismantle an independent nation and turn it into an interdependent member state of a global order is not an easy task, even with control of the media. To preside over the sell-off of a country's economic assets and public utilities, and to convert it into a site on the world map open for global exploitation without the people objecting would require a far better statesman than John Howard, someone with the charisma of Bill Clinton perhaps. To understand why, it is instructive to review the whole globalisation programme.

(a) It means the government floating the currency and removing all obstructions to the free flow of money in and out of the country, which facilitates the international exploitation of the country and its resources, including human 'resources'.

(b) It means the government ensuring global ownership of Australian industries, banks, and farms, by Transnational Corporations (TNCs) and international investors.

(c) It means the government selling all public assets and utilities to TNCs and international investors.

(d) It means the government signing away the right to control the activities of TNCs and foreign investors in exploiting Australia's resources and people, including not taxing their profits, through agreements such as the FSIA and MAI.

(e) It means getting the country into debt and keeping it there, operating thereafter on debt finance from international sources, depending on foreign investment for all future development which will be owned by the foreign investors, not Australian nationals.

(f) It means removing all protection for Australian-owned small/medium sized businesses and farms against imports from other countries including those with cheaper labour and production costs; which in turn means forcing Australian workers to compete with Asian workers for jobs in an unregulated global labour market.

(g) It means the government assisting in the destruction of the union movement so that Australian wage rates and working conditions can be more easily driven down.

(h) It means winding back the welfare state erected since the 1960s, leaving a minimum 'welfare net' and leaving Australians largely to fend for themselves in the human 'market'.

(i) It means the government signing treaties which progressively hand over Australia's political and legal sovereignty and independence to 'institutions of global governance' (world government), which are in no way accountable to the Australian people.

(j) It means the government agreeing under treaties to disarm the country and its citizens making resistance to globalisation by force impossible.

(k) It means the government agreeing to impose on the Australian people globally determined social, cultural and environmental

agendas, by having the Governor-General sign treaties at the United Nations using the questionable 'royal prerogative', and without recourse to the parliament.

(l) It means the government undertaking to 'globalise' the national culture through 'multiculturalism'.

(m) It means the media lying to the people as to what it's all about until it is too late for them to stop it.

The fate facing Australian telecommunications is another example of deregulation in action – it was formalised in July 1997. The hold up of the full-sale of Telstra in the Senate has provided whoever is driving the break up of Australia's strong public telecommunications industry (probably a mix of interests including News Corporation) with a headache.

Ever since Colston voted *"no"* to the sale the Coalition have tried to kick start the sale after the industry was deregulated.

Australian's are now being told that Telstra will lose value if it is not sold off because it cannot compete in its current form in the new deregulated industry against foreign-owned competitors. The Australian public shareholders were never being given the opportunity to comment on the changing status of the industry or the impact that it would have on their asset.

At the Institute of Public Administration Conference in Perth in September 1998 Brian Toohey said[27],

"For 20 years or so, we've been told that debate about public policy was divided into those who were economic rationalists and those who weren't. This had the convenient consequence of winning the debate before it even began. It wasn't much of a choice. Rational beats irrational any day of the week. By definition, if you weren't with the 'economic rationalists' you were irrational."

Toohey then goes on to describe how Rupert Murdoch's Fox TV has already got its hooks into Telstra – with the Australian tax payer subsidising Fox through the arrangement that it has been able to conclude with our telecommunications giant.

One does not have to think to hard about who is pushing hardest for the complete sale of Telstra... Toohey says,

"Because it is not really feasible for its competitors to replicate Telstra massive investment in infrastructure, its competitors still need access to its network. As a result the government has had to impose tough regulations to ensure that its competitors get a fair

---

[27] http://www.wa.ipaa.org.au/publications/Toohey.html

access to its network. In a speculator example where access was not even an issue, the former regulator, Austel, stopped Telstra from dropping some STD prices because it would have made it harder for Optus to build a bigger market share.

"Working out what's fair, of course, is not simple. It depends on estimates of Telstra's sunk and recurrent costs which are difficult to estimate. There is an inherent danger that the regulator, the Australian Competition and Consumer Commission, will get it wrong and be either too tough or too lenient. If it's too lenient, competition will be harmed. If it is too tough, Telstra will not be able to get a reasonable return on its investment.

"The much better solution would be to split Telstra up into a network operator and a service provider. The privatised service provider could then compete on equal terms with all the other services providers seeking access to the network.

"But many free market enthusiasts who would normally support such a split seem to have been so keen on pushing privatisation as synonymous with reform that they have overlooked the anti-competitive features at the core of the current privatisation arrangements.

"I also find it hard to justify how Telstra, when it was still a fully publicly owned body, getting into bed with a global media baron, Rupert Murdoch, to provide content for pay-TV. This concern remains after partial privatisation, given all the obvious conflicts of interest this opens up for a government wanting to maximise the return on its own shareholding as well as that of the Mum and Dad punters. Moreover, if Telstra took a half interest in a newspaper, I suspect it would raise a few eyebrows in terms of the implications for editorial control.

"As you know, every time you make a phone call in Australia you cross-subsidise Foxtel, Murdoch's pay TV joint venture with Telstra. Murdoch is not some rube who lives in the Australian bush but in metropolitan Los Angeles. So doubtless we are hearing howls of outrage from those who usually lead the charge against cross-subsidies. Not so! Australia's competition "guru" Professor Fred Hilmer has actually praised this arrangement in one of the odder arguments put forward by anyone holding a chair at an Australian University. Essentially, Hilmer argues the cross subsidy is fine because if funds the duplication, or triplication, of telephone and TV cables and so adds to competition.

Deregulation

"Hilmer rejects his own model of open access when it comes to telecommunications infrastructure. On ABC Radio on May 1, 1996, Hilmer said that going with a single cable would be the same as insisting that only Jumbo jets be allowed to fly on Australian air routes. It is a astonishing analogy. No one is suggesting anything like this, any more than they are suggesting that only one brand of truck be allowed to use Australian highways, or that only one trucking company be allowed on the roads. The more appropriate comparison for the duplication of the cable would be to argue that each airline should build and operate its own separate airport, with its own runways, control tower, fire trucks, fuel lines etc. Oddly enough, when it comes to other public utilities such as electricity, not even Hilmer has been silly enough to suggest that each generator to run it own set of power lines down suburban streets.

"Instead of increased efficiency of resource allocation — the promised outcome of competition policy — there is an extremely strong likelihood that billions of dollars will be wasted as a result of the Pay TV fiasco. Nor will the losers only be private shareholders as Hilmer implied in his ABC interview. We will all lose because the price of a phone call will be higher than would otherwise be the case."

The issues:

Deregulation is little more a legal tool used by big business to break down and destroy competition from the unwanted local small business sector.

The government portrays deregulation as a necessary step towards our entry into the globalised economy. No discussion, debate or involvement of the people most effected by deregulation in a particular industry is allowed. It is fete accompli when it happens.

When public entities like Telstra are deregulated or privatised there is no full disclosure of the main beneficiaries because the media in this country is so concentrated – and in the case of Telstra is the big beneficiary.

The truth is that the small business sector is the largest employer in Australia and that the government is hell-bent on destroying it.

The simple question that should be asked is why?

What the major parties think about this issue:

Deregulation

The major political parties have both embarked on a season of unrelenting deregulation of industry and services – mainly in the public area. It matters little whether the Coalition or the Labor party are at the helm the process continues unimpeded.

The Hilmer report is used as the government's unquestioned bible. It is interesting to note Hilmer's current position at the top of Fairfax as Brian Power's right hand man.

How the media have reported on this issue:

The media report deregulation as *"good for Australia"* and necessary to get this country into the *"global arena"*. Once again the major benefactors of deregulation are not the Australian people but the multinationals that want to do business in this country for a cold profit motive.

Is there a solution:

Regulation is the strongest safeguard for small business.

When you take it away you allow big business to swallow up competing businesses. Big business has enormous financial might and can fight long and protracted legal battles until such time as they have financially destroyed their competition.

An example of the impact of deregulation on small business is the removal of bans on late night and Sunday trading on major retailers in Western Australia. This move has all but destroyed many profitable news agents who depended on the business that they got after these retailers closed.

With regulation on business hours being returned to where they were these small businesses would have a chance to compete once again.

Chapter 8
Political Correctness

Housewife - Replaced by *Domestic Engineer.* Broken Home - Replaced by *Dysfunctional family.*

Background:

Political Correctness, says that all history is determined by power, by which groups defined in terms of race, sex, etc., have power over which other groups. Nothing else matters.

In Political Correctness certain groups are good – *feminist women,* (only feminist women, non-feminist women are deemed not to exist) *blacks, Hispanics, Jews and homosexuals.* These groups are determined to be *"victims",* and therefore automatically good regardless of what any of them do. Similarly, *"white males"* are determined automatically to be evil.

The birth pangs of political correctness can be traced back to the days when feminism first started and the time when it became common for "Ms" to replace "Mrs" or "Miss" - because the identification of a woman's marital status was seen as sexist[28].

Since these times political correctness has spread across all areas of our lives like a cancer with the backbone of each area being a powerful minority interest group with its claws in a number of committees or bureaucracies from which it receives its financial life line.

In some areas it has become entrenched that these bureaucracies have blossomed and spread their seed into a range of sub-bureaucracies. A classic example is Australia's *Department of Immigration and Multicultural Affairs.*

Political correctness hides behind the new regulators in this country. These divisive, media-supported, regulators are given extraordinary powers and a considerable amount of government funding behind which these bureaucracies are made viable. Bureaucracies whose very livelihood depends on seeking out perpetrators of crimes based on new age moral values imposed on the general population.

Among the largest politically correct institutions in Australia is the Human Rights and Equal Opportunities Commission (HREOC)

---

[28] http://www.gwb.com.au/gwb/news/onenation/pc.htm

which, despite its fancy title, is anything but what it proclaims to be.

HREOC has spawned a myriad of politically correct industries and bureaucracies all feeding off each other and depending on one another and the media for their public profile, justified existence and assault on equity and fairness in this country.

Many politically correct issues are now taboo areas for politicians to discuss. The war against the politically incorrect is now fought by the front line media. The media label those who would dare challenge these industries by terms such as *"racist"*.

In reality, organisations like HREOC are closed shops where certain people, based on sex and skin colour, are excluded from getting a fair hearing. A white male, uniquely, cannot be represented by HREOC if he is sexually discriminated against – an exclusion not faced by his white female or non-white counterpart.

It is practically impossible for a Caucasian person to take a person of another race to HREOC for racial discrimination or a race-based complaint. Consider that scenario when comparing to the basis in which HREOC actively pursue cases, on the flimsiest of evidence, where the roles are reversed.

Australia is not alone in the challenges being presented by political correctness. These challenges include what is today called affirmative action.

Like the example above of HREOC's handling of complaints of "racism" affirmative action is a classic example of political correctness in action.

This offshoot of political correctness is being addressed by the equivalent of community based referenda in many states of the USA. The first was in California where proposition 209 was adopted.

Bureaucrats and judges had previously ruled in the US that protected minorities were entitled to their fair share of the slots, and fair share came to be defined as race and gender proportion. Anything less was proof of discrimination. To avoid costly discrimination suits, employers and universities adopted a system of quotas that hired, promoted and admitted *"protected minorities"* independently of the evidence of merit to which white males were held.

After a couple of decades of quotas, equality in the law - the original civil rights goal – was replaced by *privilege in the law.*

Political Correctness

After nearly a year-long battle in the courts, California began introducing the new law, Proposition 209, that eliminated race and sex as factors in a variety of state programs from hiring to education and contracting.

The measure made California the first state in the country to abolish affirmative action programs, a move that has now captured the interest of public officials nationwide in the face of growing pressure to scrap or limit racial preferences. Campaigns for similar bans are now underway in several other states of the US.

A coalition of civil rights groups fought the will of the people in various federal courts, arguing that the law abolished programs that only benefited women and minorities while keeping preferences for those who sought them on such grounds as age, disability or veteran status.

The ultimate irony was that the politically correct American Civil Liberty Union's (ACLU) presented a case to have Proposition 209 ruled unconstitutional because it *prohibited racial discrimination.* Luckily it failed in its quest. What the ACLU had clearly demonstrated was that *"ethnic diversity"* or affirmative action is merely racism in a politically correct disguise.

While the US is removing the failed affirmative action strategy Australia is just starting to embrace it, with Tracey Carpenter heading up the new Affirmative Action Agency[29] which falls under the umbrella of the Department of Employment, Workplace Relations and Small Business.

One of Ms Carpenter's main roles is to *establish a Board consisting of people with expertise and experience in the field of Affirmative Action/Equal Employment Opportunity.*

The Aboriginal and Torres Strait Islander Commission, in a classic case of reverse racism, is allowed to blandly advertise for staff of *"Aboriginal or Islander descent"*. In other words do not apply if you do not fall into these racial groups.

Finally, the influence of the extremist international Zionist lobby, the B'nai B'rith Anti-Defamation League (ADL) should not be underestimated for their influence in pushing political correctness. The ADL is very publicly represented by the Mark Leibler headed

---

[29] http://www.dwrsb.gov.au/regplan/1999plans/AAA.htm

Australia/Israel Review[30] (AIR). ADL represents a tiny minority of Jews around the world and has a clear political agenda.

The ADL still remains as US Senator Jack B Tenney succinctly once described it, *"The largest and most efficient private gestapo in the world today and, without doubt, the largest of its kind in the history of the world. And... amazing as it may be – this vast interlocking system of departments, sections and divisions is devoted to but one issue – and only one issue despite propaganda to the contrary – political conquest in the name of Racism."*

It was ADL which established the infamous *"Racewatch"*[31] campaign with Community Aid Abroad in mid-1998 to watch for *"racist"* comments by political candidates during the Federal Election campaign. Racewatch was seen by most as a kangaroo court[32].

The issues:

Political correctness has highlighted divisions in Australia and placed a focus on them. Instead of *"curing"* these divisions, which might be race based, it has added a new dimension of confrontation and inequity to an already complex situation. It has the end result of putting a spotlight onto an area which once played no part in the Australian society.

Today political correctness reaches out to international organisations like the UN calling on this body to act as *"policeman"* over the wishes of mainstream Australia.

Political correctness and affirmative action have already been proven to be counter productive and impose impositions that the will of the majority object to. Despite this Australia seems to be plunging head long into the trap the US is busy trying to extract itself from.

What the major parties think about this issue:

The major parties are today scared of this monster that they have created yet they continue to feed it.

Deputy Prime Minister Tim Fischer hit the nail on the head when he said recently, *"Where are they going to take the action you are*

---

[30] The magazine which, in 1998, published the 2,000 One Nation members names without permission under the headline *"Gotcha"*.

[31] Racewatch, despite the media hype never ousted one "racist".

[32] http://www.gwb.com.au/gwb/news/watch

talking about? Every international forum you can think of.... political correctness poppycock. Firstly this issue should be decided here in Australia, not elsewhere."

The Labor party has embraced political correctness – and has been the proponents of giving minority groups special rights.

How the media have reported on this issue:

Political correctness is fostered by the Murdoch/Packer press. In the US Murdoch is using multi-million dollar incentives to gain support from powerful minority groups. Through this support he is lobbying to counter cross-media ownership laws in that country. The impact of and the reasons why the people of California voted to adopt Proposition 209 outlawing affirmative action have been totally ignored by the local media – this despite the fact that Australia is embarking along this road of inequity.

Furthermore, the mainstream media inaccurately portray organisations like HREOC as bona-fide bureaucracies *helping prevent and defeat racism in this country.*

ADL pushes the media around the world to promote minority groups and its own Communist-inspired political agenda. Their representatives like *AIR's* Jeremy Jones are widely reported in a highly privileged manner. Jones wrote an article[33] in AIR and was largely quoted in the *Courier-Mail* presenting me as anti-Semitic following the publication of my book *"Murder by Media"* which exposed Mark Leibler's unsavoury side.

Is there a solution:

There should be an active and deliberate dismantling of all politically correct bureaucracies and organisations.

The influence of the UN in international treaties and agreements which are nothing more than an imposition on the rights of the Australian people to conduct their own affairs as they like should be broken.

If Australians are to regain their own rights as an independent people these international scams have to be removed like the warts that they are – just simply removed.

---

[33] "Always Conspiracy": http://members.tripod.com/balson/air.htm

Chapter 9
Multiculturalism

> Supporting official multiculturalism does not mean a compassionate tolerance of the diversity of the people whom we invited to our Land, but instead means government-sponsored programs that allow some immigrants to build power bases to promote and extend their own cultures and values, while ignoring the values and ideals of the culture that invited them here.

Background:

Multiculturalism is a product of political correctness and the pursuit of minority votes in marginal seats by the number men in the major political parties – in particular the Labor Party.

This growing cancer is not unique to Australia – it has been growing across the industrialised *"Christian"* world disrupting the values and standards which these countries once held dear.

To challenge the concept of *"multiculturalism"* is to be immediately labelled a racist – when in fact, as you will see, the reverse is true.

The divisive multiculturalism debate is an ideology being foisted upon us by the media, ADL and the politicians.

Australia appears to be the only country in the Asian region embarking on this policy of encouraging cross-cultural immigration here. Ethnic-based communities supported through government funded bureaucracies. This encourages each unique culture to retain its unique profile within this country and to form enclaves. This policy extends to the retention of their own language within English speaking Australia through a kaleidoscope of multicultural radio stations and, of course, SBS television *"the multicultural station"*. One has to look no further than the Balkans in Europe to see where this road leads.

Asia has made it clear that it doesn't want whites. Asian countries such as China and Japan exclude almost all white applicants as permanent settlers or citizens because both have *"racist"* immigration policies designed to retain their racial homogeneity.. While Chinese come in greater numbers into Australia it is all one way traffic. An Asian immigrant to Australia (Miss G Lee) was recently reported in The Australian as stating, *"I am Asian and arrived in Australia in 1976. People like Al Grassby cause problems for us. I am very happy here, but I know I will never be accepted by real Australians. I do not blame them - after all their families pioneered and developed this country. They are not welcome in Asia either and cannot live there permanently."*

But this attitude of Asian nations is not seen as racist policy. In those countries it is referred to as *"positive discrimination"*. We live in a strange world, because if we are indeed part of the Asian region we better start playing to their rules or lose our identity.

The issues:

Many people have a very superficial view of racism. They see it as merely the belief that one race is superior to another. It is much more than that. It is a fundamental (and fundamentally wrong) view of human nature. Racism is the notion that one's race determines one's identity. It is the belief that one's convictions, values and character are determined not by the judgment of one's mind but by one's anatomy or *"race"* leading to a feeling of superiority over other races.

This view causes people to be condemned *(or praised)* based on their racial membership. Yet this racial division is the main pillar of *"multiculturalism"*. This division leads ethnic groups to condemn or praise others on the same basis. As a result of multiculturalism racial groups gain an authentic sense of pride not from their own achievements but from inherited characteristics. It clearly separates people along clearly defined cultural lines.

The Australian government spends hundreds of millions of dollars shoring up *"multiculturalism"* for groups such as the Chinese in Australia. Compare that support to the comparative financial starvation of the traditional Australian psyche or culture. The traditional high standard of living enjoyed by this country and the laid-back attitude of *"she'll be right"* of the okker Aussie has now been under growing threat by globalists for years.

Multiculturalism, in its purest form, spreads racism because it allows individuals to seek a sense of identity by clinging to some group, *abandoning his autonomy and his rights,* allowing his ethnic group to tell him what to believe. This is the antithesis of assimilation, or the bonding of immigrants into the general community at large. Multiculturalism promotes the individual as a *"racial entity",* he feels "himself" only among others of the same race. He becomes a separatist, choosing his friends and enemies based on ethnicity. This separatism is the basis of much of the multicultural industry in Australia.

This multicultural industry claims that its goal is to extinguish racism and build tolerance of differences. This is a complete sham. One cannot destroy the prevailing national culture while promoting that of others based on race or skin colour skin colour and then expect the victims of multiculturalism and the active participants to become colour-blind. One cannot preach the need for self-esteem while destroying the faculty which makes it possible. One cannot teach collective identity and expect individuals within cultural groups to have self-esteem.

Those who are pushing multiculturalism are, in fact, the true racists in the basic meaning of that term: *they see the world through coloured lenses, coloured by race and gender*. To the multiculturalist, race is what counts — for values, for thinking, for human identity in general.

The reason racism is increasing has nothing to do with issues being raised by Pauline Hanson and a growing number of Australians. Quite simply *"colourblindness"* is now considered evil, if not impossible. No wonder people don't treat each other as individuals - to the influential multiculturalist, they aren't.

The bureaucracies, politicians and minority groups push the claim that multiculturalism will teach the mainstream population to tolerate and celebrate their differences. *But the "differences" they have in mind are racial differences, which means we're being urged to glorify race, which means we're being asked to institutionalise separatism. "Racial identity"* erects an unbridgeable gulf between people, as though we are different species, with nothing fundamental in common. If that were true, if *"racial identity"* determined one's values and thinking methods there would be no possibility for understanding or cooperation among people of different races.

Multiculturalists claim that because the real world is diverse, and that Australian society should reflect this – even though this is to the detriment of the culture of the mainstream population. It does not appear to matter what happens to this unique Australian culture.

The existence of *"political correctness"* blasts the pretence of valuing real diversity. What these new bureaucracies want is abject conformity.

What the major parties think about this issue:

Multiculturalism

Paul Sheehan, author of *"Amongst the Barbarians"* had this to say about multiculturalism and immigration[34] in the Sydney Morning Herald, (31/5/98):

The porous welfare and immigration systems were supplemented by direct payments to ethnic organisations. Des Moore, a former deputy secretary of the Treasury and now director of his own think-tank in Melbourne, the Institute of Private Enterprise, estimates that in Labor's last full year in office, the Federal Government spent at least $143 million in direct grants to ethnic communities. ***Ninety-seven per cent of these grants went to organisations in Labor electorates.***

To distract scrutiny from this, Labor has systematically played the race card. A classic example occurred this month when the Nine Network's Sunday program was about to expose ethnic branch stacking in Melbourne. Before the program went to air, Sunday received a warning from the ALP:

Based on the information we have received, your program . . . has created the impression within some branches of the ALP that it is acting in a politically biased, if not racist, way and the ALP State Office has been asked to consider whether there have been breaches of racial discrimination and privacy laws."

The letter was signed by John Landers, State secretary of the Victorian ALP. The threat was real enough. The ability to accuse people of racism was the final, crucial, element in Labor's race strategy. Under Australia's plethora of anti-discrimination laws, a large bureaucratic machinery exists to process accusations of racism.

The Labor Party make this policy claim,

Labor remains committed to seeing Australian communities taking concrete, meaningful action, shaped and implemented at the local level to celebrate Australia's cultural diversity and to combat racism and intolerance. Labor's anti-racism campaign will highlight Australia as a country that incorporates multiculturalism, equal rights, reconciliation and non-discrimination. It will celebrate the Australian values of "a fair go", mateship and tolerance. The campaign will be funded by Government and driven by the community.

Kim Beazley told a meeting of Ethnic Communities in Melbourne in July 1998,

---

[34] http://www.gwb.com.au/gwb/news/298/3105.html

Multiculturalism

"Migrants arriving in Australia, particularly those arriving as refugees, need the security that a supportive community can give them. I place on record today Labor's enormous admiration for the Migrant Resource Centres, the ethno-specific organisations, and other community organisations that are so important to making immigrants feel at home when they first arrive in Australia.

"That welcome is crucially important to how immigrants perceive their new home, and the organisations that provide that welcome deserve security.

"This is why I announce today that a Labor Government will guarantee funding on a three-yearly basis to the Community Grants Programme to assist humanitarian entrants and migrants to settle in Australia.

"We believe in strengthening the role of these organisations as the best way of ensuring that different migrants get the particular support that they need. For some, torture and trauma counselling is vital. For others there is a stronger need to organise transitory accommodation, or language classes, and any number of other services."

The Coalition have been slightly more reserved about openly embracing multiculturalism. This changed in August 1998 when the large and wealthy Chinese lobbies in Sydney made their views clear with a stern warning to the Liberal party that they would withhold financial support and recommend to their community that they vote Labor. This ultimatum was made when the Liberal Party refused to came out strongly against Pauline Hanson's One Nation party. The Chinese lobbies demanded that Prime Minister John Howard put One Nation last on their how to vote cards. The Coalition folded and the Chinese lobby reciprocated by supporting the Liberal Party in key seats.

Just months later, in March 1999, the new deputy leader of the New South Wales Liberal Party, Mr Barry O'Farrell, went as far as to blame *"our white supremacists in Canberra"* (the Federal Liberal party) for having lost Asian voters for nearly a generation.

How the media have reported on this issue:

The media present the picture that multiculturalism somehow *"allows Australians to celebrate cultural diversity"*. Anyone who says anything different like Prof Geoffrey Blaney is persecuted as a racist for expressing the obvious.

Multiculturalism

The Murdoch/Packer media have put a loose cap on the issue of multiculturalism – many Australians continue to inwardly boil over the racist policy but fear stepping out of line because of the ramifications that they will face in the press. One can only hope that when the cap finally blows Australia will retain one of its greatest qualities – acceptance of ethnic diversity.

Is there a solution:

The only way to eradicate racism in Australia is to scrap racist programs and the philosophic frameworks, built around political correctness and multiculturalism, that feed racism.

Racism will become an ugly memory only when we embrace a valid concept of human nature. This must be based on the tenets that the individual's mind is competent, that the human intellect is efficacious, that we possess free will.

That individuals are to be judged as individuals.

That deriving one's identity from one's race to the exclusion of the community at large is a corruption - a corruption appropriate to Nazi Germany, not to a nation based on freedom and independence.

Multiculturalism needs to be scrapped and all government funding aimed at specific minority groups (most commonly to be found in marginal political seats) needs to be withdrawn and re-directed at supporting assimilation within this community.

Chapter 10
The Gay And Lesbian Lobby:

Background:

Australia was built on Christian values. These values were the foundation of this country's success. Today, there is no doubt, that these values are under threat.

Gay and lesbian behaviour is today *"accepted as normal"* by the media and is presented by well-placed gay and lesbian commentators as *"acceptable"* behaviour.

This is, of course, not the case – but it is a politically correct issue.

In recent years a series of factors have seen the gay and lesbian lobbies pushing their unwanted barrow into the homes of mainstream Australians. These include:

- The obsession that the Australian Broadcasting Corporation's television station appears to have in pushing a gay and lesbian lifestyle.
- Events like the much-publicised Sydney Mardi Gras which now includes representation by gays in the Uniting Church and even the New South Wales police.

If you object to gay and lesbian behaviour today you are called a *"homophobe"* as if you are the one who is sick, when in reality, the reverse is true – because this behaviour is not normal.

Unfortunately, gay and lesbian groups have become extremely influential today and have powerful politically correct friends, like Labor MP Cheryl Kernot, who has pushed the barrow for *"equal recognition"* of gay couples with the traditional family unit.

In 1997 the anti-discrimination tribunal fined a medical organisation Au$7,500 because they refused to put a lesbian on an IVF program.

Deputy Prime Minister Tim Fischer said at the time, *"I am totally opposed to the ruling - an extension of the IVF program - in effect to treat perfectly fertile females in many cases, something never intended in the program.*

"The comment in the ruling that there has been indirect discrimination because the form dared to refer to a male partner or husband takes the cake.

"This is building on the subtle chic trend in the tribunal industry to denigrate the family and particularly the role of males.

The Gay And Lesbian Lobby

"Enough is enough.

"Gay and lesbian couples ought to be free to lead peaceful lives but they do not have an unfettered right to gatecrash the challenge of children and deep down society knows the dangers involved."

Yet the unnatural behaviour of gays and lesbians is treated so seriously that we now have the Democrats, Greens and Labor parties pushing the Spindler Bill in the senate.

The Spindler Bill endorses a draconian ban on free speech about homosexuality in *(Clause 26)*, which prohibits expressing *"severe ridicule"* about homosexuals or transsexuals. It also prohibits *"harassment"*, defined to include anything likely to offend or insult a homosexual and *by making it unlawful* to refuse to acknowledge as normal the preferred gender of a transsexual. *If a bloke says he's a sheila, then you break the law if you say he is a bloke*!

The definition of *"harassment"* is, incredibly, a refusal to *"accept bisexuality as a distinct sexuality"*. This recommendation mandates the acceptance of an ideological position on bisexuality. It not only violates the beliefs of religious people of all faiths who regard *'bisexuality'* as a fancy word for *'depravity'*, but also shows the extent to which the McKiernan report is an exercise in sexual engineering and thought control.

The report also endorses the legal recognition of male homosexual and lesbian couples, as well as couples where one or both persons are transgender, as equal to male-female couples. While recognising that the Marriage Act may be temporarily exempt from this requirement, other Commonwealth laws would have to be amended or interpreted to reflect this profound changes forced by the Spindler Bill when passed in the Senate. The Sexual Discrimination Act 1984 which deal with marital status, for example, would now provide the recognition of homosexual couples giving them full access to IVF and to adopting children.

Intent is held by the McKiernan report to *be irrelevant in an allegation of discrimination* which, like beauty, is in the eye of the beholder - or that of the gay or lesbian complainant.

Similarly, the report recommends a prohibition, when making employment decisions, on taking into account any manner of dress which may be suggestive of a particular sexuality. So employers will just have to hire a bloke who turns up for work in drag or in full leathers and chains with exposed buttocks.

Hypothetically, under The Spindler Bill, the Anglican Church could not refuse to accept a cross-dresser as a priest, neither could it prevent him from expressing his *"sexuality"* by cross-dressing when taking a church service.

The husband of a woman who works in a West Australian hospital lamented,

My wife is a Theatre Sister and in her work she is increasingly at risk from Aids and Hep C infections which unfortunately and alarmingly are becoming more prevalent in society. A fairly large proportion of sufferers of these terrible and very contagious diseases are homosexual and I would not wish these illnesses on my worst enemy. However many homosexuals choose not to disclose their conditions to medical personnel which in term places not only their health at risk but their families as well. Hospital staff now as a rule of thumb are forced to treat every patient as potential threats to themselves. By law it is an infringement on civil liberty to be forced to declare a communicable disease to medical personnel, many unfortunately choose not to declare and thus jeopardise the health and well being off staff. I hope Josh that you would consider having this law changed so that health workers can the take extra precautions, safer with the prior knowledge of any conditions that could seriously threaten their rights to a healthy life."

The gay and lesbian lobby have found some strange bed-fellows with the Queensland Family Planning service. Its latest proposal encourages teachers to talk about *"homosexual role models"* during class at school and to hang posters depicting the Sydney Mardi Gras on the walls of the classroom. The Family Planning service are recommending this to combat *"homophobia"*.

The government department's proposal includes the incorporation of references to homosexuals in history into the curriculum. Those suggested include the queer tendencies of Oscar Wilde, Milchelangelo and Virginia Wolfe being incorporated as part of *"motivational"* strategies which would include the use of gay posters.

Under the proposal teachers would be taught to watch for *"homophobic"* behaviour including comments, name calling, ridicule and violence.

The Family Planning Queensland's Family Planning School Education co-ordinator, Judy Rose, when trying to defend the indefensible said, *"Gay and lesbian school kids have a right to enjoy being at school and a right to know there have been positive role models throughout history.*

"Maybe you are studying Oscar Wilde and you say he was gay, it is an important fact that had an impact on his writings.

"What we are looking at first of all is addressing homophobia and further down the track we will get into the area of celebrating diversity."

Workshops styled *"Out with Homophobia"* were launched in April 1999 as a voluntary programme for school teachers.

"There is no point in stirring things up and creating anxiety in the community by being provocative," Rose said. *"We have to be really careful about the way it is handled, they are being harassed now."*

A bit of sense is brought back into the argument with Ben de Jong, a spokesman for the Family Council of Queensland, saying that schools were not there to promote a homosexual lifestyle, *"I don't think that should come from the teacher. Obviously they don't question every teacher to find out what their lifestyle is."*

Predictably the state Labor government's position is to side with the gays. A spokeswoman for Education Minister Dean Wells said, *"Schools should be about fostering tolerance via the anti-Discrimination Act and anti-bullying programmes."*

The issues:

Please note the explicit and frank language used in this section is included for the sole reason of debunking the myth that gay and lesbian behaviour is *"normal"*.

Gay and lesbian behaviour is not normal. The manner in which it is promoted on television, in the media and soon in some Queensland schools is a travesty of justice and an attack on the traditional family.

Boys and girls are particularly vulnerable as they reach the age of puberty. The introduction of open discussion in the classroom glorifying a queer lifestyle is an enormously damaging move on good Christian values.

This is how Dr E R Fields summed up the practices of the gay population[35]. This information is carried to totally refute the idea that queer behaviour should be promoted in schools as *"normal"* and *"acceptable"*:

ORAL SEX is practiced by all homosexuals. In most such acts, they ingest semen. Semen contains the same germs carried in the

---

[35] http://members.localnet.com/~bobg/ifa25.htm

blood system. As a result, consuming semen poses the same risk to health as would the consumption of raw human blood.

ANAL SEX is practiced by 90% of the homosexuals and two-thirds participate regularly according to the Corey and Holmes study. The group studied had an average of 110 different sex partners and 68 rectal encounters per year.

During anal intercourse, the rectum becomes a mixing bowl of saliva, faeces, semen and all of the germs from these sources. Since the rectal wall is only one cell thick, tearing of the anal wall frequently occurs allowing direct access to the blood stream of these contaminants. This can also transmit Hepatitis B, another deadly communicable disease that can be easily transmitted to innocent people through food service, a favourite career of homosexuals.

FAECAL SEX is practiced by 80% of gays. They lick or insert their tongues into the anuses of partners and ingest faeces. Half of these admit to such loathsome practices on a regular basis. Dr. J. Elford of London in his 1992 study found that homosexuals continued this practice, which they call *"Rimming"* at the same level as in his 1984 study.

This practice of ingesting faeces is the chief cause of Hepatitis and parasitic infections common among homosexuals. According to the San Francisco Department of Public Health, 70 to 80% of that city's 75,000 cases of hepatitis are among homosexuals. The Centers for Disease Control issued a report on hepatitis among gays and found that they are carriers of this disease in 29% of the cases in Denver, 66% in New York, 56% in Toronto, 42% in Montreal and 26% in Melbourne. Hepatitis is highly communicable and is spread by unsanitary conditions. It kills by destroying the liver. Innocent people are in danger of hepatitis infection from gays who work in great numbers as cooks and waiters at restaurants.

Medical authorities, writing in publications oriented to homosexuals, named the chronic infection of gays with various intestinal parasites the *"Gay bowl syndrome"*.

Similarly, the eating of faeces has been blamed for causing typhoid fever, herpes and cancer. Some 10% of gays admit to the practice of deliberately eating faeces and/or drinking contaminated enema water!

ANONYMOUS SEXUAL ENCOUNTERS or *"one night stands"* with strangers in public restrooms is practiced by 41% of gays while 60% commit such acts with strangers in so-called

"Bathhouses". During these already high-risk encounters, some 64% admit to using illegal drugs. In one study of 824 promiscuous gays, Dr. Steven Morin found that the media-promoted *"Safe Sex"* campaign resulted in their reducing their appetite down from an average of 70 to 47 sexual encounters per year.

SADOMASOCHISM is the pastime for 37% of homosexuals. This is giving or receiving torture for sexual pleasure. Many deaths in cities with a large gay population have been attributed to *"accidental"* strangulations and related causes during the course of a session of S & M sex. In San Francisco concerned medical authorities felt it necessary to conduct, at taxpayer expense, classes in sadism and masochism for gays in the belief that it would prevent accidental deaths. In such cases, they learned how to tie up a partner without cutting off circulation.

URINE SEX is practiced by 29% of gays who call it *"Golden Showers"*. This is drinking or being splashed with urine, a highly toxic substance. Death can occur from urine consumption.

IN SUMMARY: A Corey and Holmes study in Seattle during 1992 found that the average homosexual in one year sodomised 108 males and swallowed semen from 48 of them. They allowed 68 males to penetrate their anus with the penis and ingested faeces from 19 partners. Not surprisingly, during the period of this study 10% contracted hepatitis B and 7% got hepatitis A.

This is not normal behaviour, never has been and never will be. The unsanitary activities practised lead to some 78% of gays contracting sexually transmitted diseases. Depending on the city, some 30% to 59% have been infected with intestinal parasites such as worms, flukes and amoebae.

Finally, when I was a young lad, when we talked about a *"gay"* time we were talking about a happy time. Today the straight population dare not use that word because it has been prostituted to represent the queer antics of homosexuals in our community.

What the major parties think about this issue:

Both the major parties have embraced gay and lesbian behaviour as normal. The Labor party, in particular, is a big proponent of the gay scene and fully endorses the Spindler Bill currently before the senate.

The Liberal Party have some concerns about the length that the Spindler Bill goes to but do not appear to outraged at the general thrust of the document. Deputy Prime Minister Tim Fischer has been particularly outspoken about the politically correct aspect behind gay and lesbian behaviour.

How the media have reported on this issue:

The media glorify homosexual behaviour. Many reporters today fall into this category and carefully guard the reputation of their sexual deviancy. The theme of coverage by the media is most often based around *"coming out"* and *"fun and enjoyment"* of this lifestyle. The reality is very different with the gay lifestyle being a very unfulfilling reality. Despite this people who present *"homophobic"* views are hammered by the media as *"narrow-minded"* and *"living in the past"*.

Is there a solution:

The simple solution is to put the queer lifestyle back behind doors where it belongs. It should not be glorified by the media and never presented as acceptable in schools.

If someone wants to embrace a homosexual relationship that should be their decision alone without outside influences through weird events like the Sydney Mardi Gras presenting it as *"fun"* and *"acceptable"*. It is not.

The truth for the victims of their own unnatural practices is far from the image presented – and HIV Aids, and Hepatitis B are just some medical outcomes that support my view that this is the case.

Chapter 11
The Republican Debate:

The controversial draft Constitutional preamble for the Australian Republic as presented by John Howard in March 1999:

With hope in God, the Commonwealth of Australia is constituted by the equal sovereignty of all its citizens.

The Australian nation is woven together of people from many ancestries and arrivals.

Our vast continent has helped to shape the destiny of our Commonwealth and the spirit of its people.

Since time immemorial our land has been inhabited by Aboriginal and Torres Strait Islanders, who are honoured for their ancient and continuing cultures. In every generation immigrants have brought great enrichment to our nation's life.

Australians are free to be proud of their country and heritage, free to realise themselves as individuals, and free to pursue their hopes and ideals. We value excellence as well as fairness, independence as dearly as mates.

Australia's democratic and federal system of government exists under law to preserve and protect all Australians in an equal dignity which may never be infringed by prejudice or fashion or ideology nor invoked against achievement.

In this spirit we, the Australian people, commit ourselves to this constitution.

Background:

The thing that worries most thinking Australians about the body leading the Republican push, the Australian Republican Movement (ARM), is the direct involvement of big business in its leadership. The ARM is funded by big business.

There are four elements to the ARM's platform these are:

1. Australia shall have a Head of State who is an Australian citizen, who is appointed by Australians and who represents the independent and sovereign nation of Australia. The Federal and State Parliaments will remain unchanged. Our governments will continue to be elected as they are now.
2. The new Head of State, to be known as *"the President of Australia"* will be chosen by Australians. The President will be able to be removed by a vote of the House of Representatives. The President will be elected for a single

five year term and must be a citizen of Australia eligible to vote.

3. The President will have the same role and powers as the Governor General. The functions of the President shall be spelled out in the Constitution and shall be no greater than those of the Governor General. The President (like the Governor General) will act on the advice of the duly elected Government unless the Government has lost the confidence of the House of Representatives or is breaking the law.
4. Australia will remain a member of the Commonwealth of Nations, most of whose members are already republics. Australia will continue to play an active role in other international and regional associations, including the United Nations.

In summary the ARM present the front that all Australians should be proud of their country and committed to its values. They state that every Australian child should be able to aspire to be our Head of State. They claim that in a diverse nation like ours it is important that everyone can identify with our national institutions and that they represent Australia, not another country. They say that as it stands today, no Australian, not matter how clever they are or how hard they work will ever be Australia's Head of State.

What they do not say is

- that big business, the men and women pushing and pulling all their levers are the same people behind the globalisation of Australia;
- that any Australian can become governor under the status-quo and
- that an Australian Republic will require the total re-writing of the Australian Constitution.

The chairman of the ARM is none other than Malcolm Turnbull, a man very closely associated with Kerry Packer. Turnbull made more than Au$50 million from the recent float of OzEmail, an Internet Service Provider. The man giving Turnbull a leg up into the big league was his mate Kerry Packer – who bought into OzEmail. Major shareholder Turnbull was chairman at the time.

Malcolm Turnbull is also a merchant banker, a smart lawyer and today, thanks to Packer, a very wealthy man. Packer has rarely, if ever, done anything for humanitarian reasons. His modus operandi is based around gambling and setting the stakes very high when it comes to returns on investments that he is involved in. He is cold blooded and callous – if an investment or its management do not come up to expectations they can expect to be given the flick. Hiring and firing, more often than not, takes place on the golf course not a boardroom table with Packer questioning his lieutenants about the performance of his businesses as they play.

For ARM to achieve their aim of making Australia a republic they have to get the people to agree to a Constitutional amendment.

Section 128 of the Constitution requires that a proposed amendment can only become law if it is approved in a referendum by a majority of voters in a majority of states, and a national majority of voters overall.

In March 1998 Australia witnessed a costly and farcical *"Republican Convention"* held in the old parliament in Canberra – at its conclusion Turnbull's big business ARM, despite massive advertising budgets pushing its case, managed just 73 votes in favour out of 152 for their preferred republican model. Not the two-thirds majority required for a referendum to be carried. On these figures, they have a huge selling task ahead of them to convince the Australian people.

Despite the two-thirds majority not being achieved *"monarchist-leaning"* Prime Minister John Howard pushed ahead with a republic referendum anyway – it will be held in November 1999.

This brings me to the huge financial incentive that is driving the foreign multinationals and rich men and women who are pushing for Australia to change from a country beholden to the Queen of Australia. Under the revised republican model the President will be selected by the Parliament not the people. The influence of big business on politicians should not be underestimated.

The track record of big business in dealing honestly with the general population is worse than abysmal as you have already seen in this book. If their rhetoric and the basis of the change providing *"all Australians an equal opportunity to become Head of State"* was true it would be a major divergence from their performance in the past.

Let us not get too hung up about the enormous costs of ripping up an entrenched system of government in this country and replacing it with another if it was good for the Australian people we should welcome it. Let us not get too hung up about why we should change a system which *"ain't broke"*. What we should be looking at is what are these bureaucrats and representatives of big business going to do to the Australian constitution?

Currently the Australian constitution:

- defines the Parliament as "the Queen, a Senate, and a House of Representatives" and vests the Federal legislative (law-making) power in the Parliament (section 1, Constitution).
- states that the executive power (the governing and administrative power) of the Commonwealth of Australia is vested in the Queen (section 61, Constitution).
- ensures that the Queen has the power to disallow any law within one year of it being made even after the Governor-General has given his assent (section 59, Constitution).
- enforces the position that the Governor-General only holds office *"at the Queen's discretion"* which means that the he can be dismissed by the Queen at any time (section 2, Constitution).
- and lastly, but probably most importantly in a symbolic sense, is the Schedule to the Constitution requires all Federal MPs to swear an oath or declare an affirmation of allegiance to the Queen. This oath of allegiance can only be changed by alteration of the Constitution unlike the Citizenship Oath which can be changed by an Act of Parliament or the Ministerial Oath which can be changed Proclamation.)

The constitution will have to be totally re-written for Australia to become a republic. Why haven't the Australian people been informed who is writing our new constitution before we vote in a Republic and when will we get a chance to see it, debate it or approve it? Will we in fact be given that opportunity? Like the MAI will *"big business"* be exclusively involved in its re-drafting?

The incredible breadth and depth of the ARM's proposed constitutional changes can be seen on the Internet at this address:
http://www.republic.org.au/const/tdraft.html

The last time that the Australian people voted on a simple *one line amendment* to the constitution the change spelt disaster. Race based parameters were recognised in our constitution in 1967 by the people after the referendum giving special status to the Aborigines. The amendment has been latched onto by the legal fraternity.

The upshot of the Referendum was: [i]s127 of the Constitution was repealed. s127 previously stated: *"In reckoning the numbers of people of the Commonwealth, or of a State or other part of the*

Commonwealth, aboriginal natives shall not be counted" and [ii]ss xxvi of s51(Legislative Powers of the Parliament) was changed to read: *["The Parliament shall, subject to this Constitution, have power to make laws for the peace, order and good government of the Commonwealth with respect to:"] "the people of any race for whom it is deemed necessary to make special laws".*

Previously, this clause had read...

["The Parliament shall, subject to this Constitution, have power to make laws for the peace, order and good government of the Commonwealth with respect to:"] "the people of any race, other than the aboriginal race in any State, for whom it is deemed necessary to make special laws".

The 1967 amendment, entrenched in the Australian constitution, now forms the *constitutional basis of legalised native title claims* and the formation of the prohibitively expensive race-based Aboriginal and Torres Strait Islander Commission. The change unwittingly recognised race above equity. When Australians voted for the change they had absolutely no idea that they were voting in a myriad of legal challenges through the modified constitution.

How many Australians would have voted for that change today if they had realised then the can of legalistic worms that they opened - as well as plunging Australia into the "race debate".

The issues:

It is my personal belief that this debate over the *"republic"* is a total red herring. The real issue driving those in the ARM and their big business mates is the re-drafting of the country's constitution which currently provides Australian sovereignty with some semblance of protection from big business globalists and their international treaties. If there is one thing for sure it is that a new republican-based constitution will open the doors so wide for globalists that Australia can kiss any remaining vestige of its sovereignty goodbye.

Stan Deyo wrote in February 1998 (during and about the constitutional convention):

I have attended by the invitations of Sir John Williams (Adelaide Steamship and Salvage) and Sir Henry Sommerset (a CSIRO chancellor) the Melbourne Club in Collins Street. I have dined there and sipped ports and smoked cigars with many of the old cotton-topped knights who are the Australian members of the "Round Table" (RIIA). There I have discussed technologies and financial and political strategies which are so far beyond the average man in the street that to even seriously ask him to believe them would be futile - much less to ask him to help defeat their control.

I have dealt with representatives of Dutch Shell Oil in North Melbourne in the old days.... I have rung Billy Sneddon at home to give him instructions regarding meetings with us and Dutch Shell Oil in a room behind Sir Robert Menzies' home in Melbourne at the time....

I would probably still be there where I was promised that I would be "properly assimilated into business and social life in Melbourne" by Sir John and Sir Henry.... IF I had followed the party line and had kept their secrets. We parted ways in 1973... I knew they were under siege by a more powerful group than their own.

Then, something happened to their powerhold in 1973-74. They were defeated by a group that was bigger and tougher on a planetary scale. I do not know if you are really aware of what you are up against. It is not simply the political leaders. It is not simply the Murdochs or the Packers. It is something with real, incredible, tangible power and the technical knowledge and the will to use it against the human race to achieve its goal.

It was in 1975 that Australia signed the Lima agreement – the new world order's blue print to globalisation.

Stan Deyo continues:

I wish it were as simple as electing good people to office; but it is not - as you must already realise. Knowing how the old Round Table used to play both sides of the fence, I am not even certain that there could ever be a truly independent political leadership in the world as long as they have power. I saw them manipulate major political parties, business groups, think tanks and political movements from the inside.

I suppose I am trying to wish you well... as well as those who help you in good faith. I know you must be feeling somewhat frustrated at times. Just try to stand by your guns as long as you can.... Things are coming to a head very rapidly on a global basis; so there is hope down the road a few kms....

Stan Deyo

What the major parties think about this issue:

The Republican Debate

The Labor Party under *"big picture"* Paul Keating pushed for Australia to become a republic. The media embraced Keating's words giving the move their blessing. This was the *"world's greatest treasurer"* who was responsible for our banks becoming convenient assets for Wall Street bankers through the FSIA.

Labor believes that the monarchy no longer reflects either the fundamental democratic principles underlying the Australian nation or its diversity. Labor believes that our Head of State should be an Australian who embodies and represents the traditions, values and aspirations of all Australians.

Labor supported Australia becoming an independent Republic prior to the Sydney Olympics in September 2000. This would have ensured that the new Australian President open the Olympic Games. Their loss at the October 1998 elections destroyed that ambition.

Labor supports the bi-Partisan Appointment Model as agreed to by the Constitutional Convention, which met in February 1998.

The bi-Partisan Appointment Model would see the President appointed following a motion before a joint sitting of both Houses of the Parliament moved by the Prime Minister and seconded by the Leader of the Opposition. The Presidential nominee would need the support of two thirds of a joint sitting of the Parliament to be appointed.

You will notice that under Labor's model and the model now being pushed by the ARM the people of Australia would have no choice in the selection of the President. (The ARM are very careful to claim that they are a-political – a convenient ploy when trying to attract non-Labor voters.).

Consider the power of the media over politicians and then think carefully about who the major beneficiaries of an Australian Republic will be.

The President could be dismissed by the Prime Minister of the day. The President would have the same powers as are currently held by the Governor-General and the Queen.

The Coalition Party, unlike the Republican-leaning Labor Party, has had its feet in both camps. Some Coalition members are died in the wool monarchists while the majority of their senior politicians believe that Australia should become a Republic.

Howard has shown his true colours after earlier claiming to be a *"monarchist"* by pushing ahead with a referendum on the Republic in November 1999. Howard said that if clear support for a particular Republican model emerged from the 1998 Convention that his government would put that model to a referendum of the Australian people before the end of 1999. This *"clear support"* replaces the previous requirement of a two-third majority.

Howard has made it known that he will *"have a hand"* in personally drafting the new constitution if the people decide to scrap the old one which has served them so well for many generations. Consider the impact of Murdoch's single bedside visit to Howard in 1997 when Packer was using Michael Kroger to try to get the media ownership laws changed to enable him to acquire Fairfax. The Coalition immediately dropped its *"mogul-specific"* plans.

If the people then decide to change our present Constitution, the new arrangements will be in place for the centenary of the inauguration of the Australian nation and the opening of the new millennium on 1 January 2001.

And we will never know who really had a hand in the revision of our constitution and its beneficial implications for big business.

How the media have reported on this issue:

The media are leaning towards the views being put forward by the ARM under the revised republican model. This represents the interests of bis business.

Is there a solution:

Quite simply, as Howard once said, *"if it ain't broke, why fix it?"* It is the Australian constitution which is the cornerstone of our society.

Why would we want anyone to re-draft it after our experiences of what happened following the referendum in 1967. If there was a flaw in our current constitution the multinationals would be exploiting it more than the have – a change will give them ample opportunity to avoid this current impediment.

Chapter 12
The Australian Media

> *"If you are rich you can say what you like and what's more, you can stop anyone else saying what you don't want heard... it's the triumph of the raw power of money"*
> Terry Lane, Free Speech Committee speaking on ABC's 7.30 Report (9/4/99)

Background:

The Australian media is in crisis. The level of control exerted on what Australians read, see and hear by just two families should ring the alarm bells in the minds of all those who believe in an open democracy.

There is no doubt that the greatest casualty of this concentration is freedom of speech and the greatest losers after the general population are today's journalists whose integrity is questioned as a result. Australians are only told what the media barons want them to know. The small independent publications like *The Strategy* and the on-line *Australian Daily Issues Paper*[36] are portrayed by Murdoch and Packer as fronts for the extreme right and are labelled as *"anti-Semitic or racist"*.

It wasn't always this way.

Many years ago Australia enjoyed a far more diverse media ownership with several large independent media groups giving different perspectives on the same issue – a very healthy outcome.

Today, under the closed shop, things are portrayed as black or white. Many areas, like the tax avoidance strategies pursued by their owners, are taboo – despite being in the public interest.

While Packer's wealth has been generated from what he would term *"smart"* business deals and tax avoidance the phenomenal growth of Murdoch's empire has been on a global scale.

Murdoch's News Group International assets include the lion's share of BSkyB; Twentieth Century Fox; major British newspapers such as The Sun, News of the World; The Times; The Sunday Times, much of America's Pay TV market, the Times Literary and Educational Supplements and most Australian papers.

---

[36] http://www.gwb.com.au/gwb/news/daily.html

Murdoch's father, Keith, although only a low paid reporter, made a fortuitous marriage to Elisabeth Joy Greene the daughter of a wealthy Jewish family. The family fortune enabled Keith Murdoch to buy himself a knighthood, a radio station and two Adelaide newspapers, as well as to educate his son Rupert at a fashionable Geelong private school and then to send him to Oxford University.

When his father died young Rupert Murdoch returned to Australia to take over the two newspapers. He borrowed millions to buy up Australian media and by 1968 his media empire was worth $46 million.

His buying spree continued throughout the 1970s. He went off-shore establishing his influence in Britain and then the United States. The last few years, with his move into satellite television pay TV and film studios, have seen Murdoch establish his influence on a global scale, with assets estimated at $14.3 billion.

Of concern is who wields the financial power over Murdoch? Consider this - 45% of trading in News Corporation occurs on the New York Stock Exchange according to The Sydney Morning Herald (22/6/95) – and Rockefeller's Chase Manhattan Nominees is one of the company's five largest shareholders.

The phenomenal rise of Murdoch is no accident. It is based on the financial backing of four mega-money moguls. Murdoch started to move in these circles when his father asked Lord Beaverbrook to train the then young Rupert in the newspaper business.

Beaverbrook introduced Murdoch to Harry Oppenheimer, head of the massive Anglo-American Corporation and Edgar Bronfman. Both men were impressed by the young Rupert Murdoch and told him to call on them if he needed help.

Within a few years Murdoch was acting as the front-man for media buy- ups financed by Oppenheimer and Bronfman, as well as being helped by Armand Hammer and the Rothschild empire. These men collectively saved Murdoch from bankruptcy in 1990 following the 1987 collapse of the global stock markets.

This almost limitless financial backing is the real force behind Murdoch's mercurial rise to control, among his other media interests, annual paper circulation of over 3.5 billion copies.

Murdoch had earlier demonstrated that he is not shy of using this enormous power to further his, and his backers' own political agenda. As far back as 1972, after Australian Labour Party leader Whitlam had agreed to pursue a 100 per-cent pro-Israeli policy and to protect Murdoch's growing empire. The power of his media was used to run a block-busting campaign which steamrollered Whitlam into power.

When Whitlam promptly reneged on the deal Murdoch's media turned on him as part of the successful campaign to have Whitlam removed from office and replaced by the fervently pro-Zionist Bob Hawke who led Australia down the current dead-end path of globalisation following the signing of the secret Lima agreement.

Like father, like son. It was Lachlan Murdoch who instructed his editorial staff around Australia to *"Kill the cow*[37]*"* just weeks before the October 1998 Federal Election. And they did. They pursued Hanson's party with relentless written and verbal vile and venom. The media, as a result, destroyed the party's credibility in the minds of many through blatantly biased reporting. The end result was many misled Australians became disenchanted with all things political.

Included on Murdoch's agenda of vilification are attacks on his enemies, among which he includes Germans, Irish, Arabs and anti-Zionists - *"the supreme traitors"*.

Last year American media mogul CNN's Ted Turner apologised to the B'nai B'rith Anti-Defamation League after likening Murdoch to Hitler, alleging that, like Hitler, Murdoch used the media outlets over which he has control to further his political agenda. Turner has promised to donate US$1 billion to the United Nations – the body behind globalisation.

There can be absolutely no argument that the power that the Packer and Murdoch families wield over government – whether it be Labor or Coalition - is quite extraordinary. These two families can, through the media, make or break the reputation of an individual politician or a party – if they do not tow the line. A classic example of this was the manner in which the mainstream media went after the *"populist"* based Pauline Hanson's One Nation party.

The media moguls can demand and get an audience with any member of the government, Labor or Coalition, at any time. Rupert Murdoch flew to Australia in August 1997 visiting a bed-bound Prime Minister John Howard.

Murdoch, Australian born but now an American citizen, made the fly-by visit to bluntly warn Howard that his government was

---

[37] In other words end the political career of Pauline Hanson.

doomed if it pursued Packer's agenda of gaining control of the Fairfax empire while excluding him, as a foreigner, from the spoils.

In the months leading up to Murdoch's visit Michael Kroger, the merchant banker and Liberal power broker, was working the corridors of power in Canberra for Packer. He was actively lobbying Communications Minister Senator Richard Alston and Treasurer Peter Costello to bow to Packer's demands which were seen by Murdoch as *"mogul specific"*.

The changes to media ownership laws being considered would exclude foreign owners (like News Corp) from the Fairfax prize but allow cross-ownership between television stations and the papers – mogul specific as Packer would be the only winner.

During these negotiations few journalists dared speak out except for The Sydney Morning Herald's Margo Kingston who said on ABC television at the time,

"The problem with Kerry Packer is that he is so powerful, the politicians aren't game enough to cross him. Look at history.

"Go back to 1991 when he and Conrad Black through Toorang wanted to take over Fairfax. He said, because of the cross-media (rules) he could only have 15% in print,

1) he said I don't control it, I won't try to control it,

2) he said foreign ownership restrictions are ridiculous, let's blow them out of the water.

"Peter Costello, then on the print-media inquiry now Packer's chief urger with Richard Alston, said back then I haven't got a problem with foreign ownership, my problem is diversity, I really care about diversity therefore I'll let foreigners in provided they don't increase concentration.

"Now, Kerry Packer has changed his mind. Now he doesn't care about media diversity and he does care about foreign ownership. He doesn't care about media diversity because he wants to take over Fairfax and keep (Channel) Nine, but he does care about foreign ownership because, guess what, he doesn't want to have any competition to buy Fairfax. The only competition comes from foreigners. And now, the government has completely switched its rhetorical and logical position and is again arguing for Mr Packer.

"Now when you have a man so powerful that he can buy Graham Richardson to talk the Labor party around and Michael Kroger to talk the Liberal party around, and Howard and Costello and Alston jump to his every need no matter how irrational, no matter how

transparently incoherent their arguments, we have a huge problem. And yes, personally I am very scared, personally, of Mr Packer taking over Fairfax."

Very few people heard Kingston's words. A different mogul-specific picture was painted by the Murdoch press just days after Murdoch's bedside visit. The verbal artillery across the bows of the Coalition government had begun sending it into panic mode.

In September 1997 *The Australian* warned:

John Howard will be the other big loser.

Having frozen out the country's largest newspaper group, News Limited, (from owning Fairfax) he has now alienated Packer's interests, which include the country's biggest magazine publishing empire and its most powerful television network, Nine.

The Courier-Mail's Peter Charlton was more forthright to the wheelings and dealings going on behind the scenes:

...they (Richard Alston and Peter Costello) also are close to Victorian Liberal powerbroker Michael Kroger whose merchant bank was handling the Packer attempt to acquire the additional Fairfax shares.

Estimates of Kroger's potential fee went as high as Au$7 million.... It is, however, fair to say that had the (Packer's) Fairfax stake been increased Kroger's merchant bank would have stood to gain handsomely.

The reason that the backroom deals were stripped bare and exposed to the public in this case was quite simple. The government was negotiating to give a power base (Fairfax) to Packer while giving Murdoch nothing in return. ***If Murdoch had been offered some financial incentive in return the Australian people would never have heard about the role of the Liberal powerbroker, Kroger, or his pending reward for negotiating the political path for the handover of Fairfax to Packer - or the story behind the changes to the media ownership laws.***

This is because the mainstream media is already so concentrated in Australia.

The Fairfax scenario outlined above happened in 1997. Today the two media barons are more closely aligned. They share major shareholdings in a number of large media enterprises. The war between them under the young lions Lachlan (Murdoch) and James (Packer) seems to have been replaced by an amnesty of sorts. This followed the act of greed before loyalty perpetrated against the Australian Rugby League (ARL) by Packer and Optus (a company in which Packer has a substantial interests). For over a year the ARL had used the high courts to fight off Murdoch's Fox Pay TV which wanted to secure the rights to running a competitive sporting event called Super League.

The ARL was able to continue the fight as long as Optus and Channel 9 supported the founding body of rugby league in the courts. Behind the scenes the Packer and Murdoch camps were fighting out the real business deals with the public face of the court case being nothing more than a handy distraction presented to the public and giving fallacious argument to what was really happening behind closed doors.

When the two parties came to an equitable agreement support for the ARL was promptly dropped by both Optus and Channel 9. Left floating without the financial support required to maintain its viability the ARL's resolve folded without so much as a whimper.

Today the ARL has been replaced by Murdoch's Fox Pay TV controlled Super League and most of the important live matches once enjoyed by Australians on free-to-air television (Channel 9) are now locked behind Fox Pay television sports channels. Packer and Murdoch were the only winners from the demise of the ARL.

Most boardroom battles are not so public – what the Packer and Murdoch camps have learnt is that these public brawlings have allowed Australians to get a key-hole glance of what is actually happening in their shadowy corridors of power.

As they control the media so effectively they have been able to keep all other deals – *which are in the public interest out of the news*. Anybody who dares raise an issue related to these wheelings and dealings, like the MAI, is shrugged off by being referred to as a *"conspiracy theorist"*.

Thousands of articles are mirrored presenting those who publicly disagree with the moguls agenda as *"uninformed"* and *"vacuous nonsense"* while their viewpoint is always intellectually *"sound"*.

The growing alliance between the Packer and Murdoch empires should be a matter of great concern to all Australians. Adverse reporting over Packer's more recent assault on the Fairfax empire has been significant by its absence in the Murdoch press.

The day that Packer's henchman Brian Powers resigned from Publishing and Broadcasting Limited in May 1998 he joined the board of Fairfax Limited. No questions were asked – even after senior staff were sacked or resigned and even though Powers, just days later, was appointed Chairman of Fairfax.

Power's position of influence came through the FXF Trust shared with Kerry Packer. Packer guaranteed Au$12 million in loans for Powers as part of the Fairfax share purchase by the FXF Trust. The guarantee by Packer allowed the FXF Trust to control just under 15% of Fairfax Limited – the maximum amount that Packer is allowed under cross-ownership laws. The trust is Fairfax's largest shareholder following the sale by New Zealand based Brierley Investments Limited (BIL) of its 23% shareholding in 1998.

The BIL sale included a *"buy-back"* of shares by Fairfax which pushed FXF's holding in the company to 16.5% of the equity in the company – *a clear breach of the media ownership laws.*

Yet, the *Australian Broadcasting Authority* (ABA) which held a year-long investigation into the FXF trust's relationship and control of the Fairfax group found in March 1999 that Packer and Powers were somehow *"innocent"* of any controlling interest.

Their decision was based on two points, one that FXF would reduce its shareholding to below the 15% mark and Packer's comment that *"What I find so extraordinary is, if I control Fairfax, do you think they'd run the stories they run about me?"*

The Chair of the ABA, Professor David Flint, said on the conclusion of their investigation into Packer's control over Fairfax, *"In considering whether to not to grant approval, the ABA took account of the fact that the breaches were the result of action by persons other than the Packer Interests. The ABA also took account of two undertakings provided to the ABA."*

The *Sydney Morning Herald* was to report just days after the ABA finding was released that the six man inquiry had changed its decision from one confirming an association between Packer, Powers and a control of Fairfax to the final resolution absolving them after receiving sternly worded letters from lawyers representing both men.

An insider close to the inquiry was to comment that the ABA changed its point of view on the Packer/Powers relationship and Fairfax *because it did not want to become in costly and lengthy court cases.*

ABA's chairman David Flint said, when questioned about the impact of the legal threats, *"The whole process requires and expects that we must receive the submissions with a completely open mind and be ready to change our positions. The fact we then change our position is not only not surprising, it is to be expected."*

The silence of the Murdoch press this time round compared to the 1997 outcry was deafening. Just this one earlier commentary by Terry McCrann in the *Courier-Mail* in December 1998 gave some insights on concerns that should be vigorously debated in public,

So there is nothing particularly significant in its (BIL) departure. Its absolute lack of influence in the Fairfax boardroom was well and truly confirmed when it ceded the chair to former Kerry Packer right-hand man Brian Powers. The sale and, more particularly the way some of the shares have been cancelled and the rest dispersed, fundamentally cements the Fairfax company within the Packer corporate orbit. Fairfax is now indisputably a Packer company.

The reason behind Murdoch's apparent disinterest this time round appears to be tied in with his new business bond with Packer and the political influence of a new member of his *"policy team"*. His name is Grahame Morris. Morris was *"sacked"* from the Prime Minister's office in October 1997 after he became entangled in the travel rorts fiasco He had, apparently, withheld information and, happily accepted his fate over 20 years as Howard's right hand man. He joined Murdoch's staff the same day he was fired.

Lachlan Murdoch said this about Morris's appointment: *"Grahame's appointment to the senior management position will strengthen News Limited's policy team. He will assist us in developing strategic plans for the future of our business and will provide additional expertise in the handling of regulatory issues."*

Just a year later word leaked out that Murdoch was at a very advanced stage of negotiation with the government in establishing a free-to-air television network or claiming Channel 7. Murdoch's interest in Channel 7 has nothing to do with the current technology but everything to do with broadband television – a bounty already handed to Kerry Packer and 7 by the Coalition following Packer's disappointment over the *"failure"* to acquire the Fairfax prize.

In March 1999 it was announced that parts of the publicly-owned Australian Broadcasting Commission (ABC) would be privatised as key Liberal powerbroker, merchant banker and newly-appointed ABC board member Michael Kroger started making an impression on the government owned media outlet. Kroger's good friend Communications Minister senator Richard Alston made the announcement on Channel 9. The privatisation followed complaints by the Liberal Party that the ABC had treated them unfairly in the lead-up to the October 1998 Federal election.

The privatisation of 50% of the sophisticated Internet side of the ABC's operations should once again ring alarm bells – but the mainstream media, waiting in the wings for another prize, have been less than forthcoming in looking at Kroger's role in this move. In fact, the media lauded Kroger's marriage to Andrew Peacock's daughter the day before Alston made the announcement as *"the social occasion of the year"*. Not surprisingly Lachlan Murdoch, James Packer, John Howard and Communications Minister Senator Richard Alston were among Kroger's handpicked party of two hundred wedding guests.

Just days after the ABC privatisation promise James Packer told a packed house at the launch of a new look *"The Bulletin"*,

"The importance of global scale and the reality of the foreign competition that our media already faces now vastly outweighs the benefits of trying to protect our media from foreign ownership."

What Packer was talking about was two things. The impact of the Internet and sending out strong signals of reconciliation to the Murdoch empire, his new partner, in an Australian media which is rapidly moving from a duopoly to an effective monopoly.

Who would stand in his way? Coincidently on the Sunday's before and after his comments Channel 9's 60 Minutes programme ran segments exposing Paul Keating and his shonky piggery deals. What would have not been understood by the mainstream Australian population viewing these claims was that Channel 9 had had this information since May 1993 – when it was raised and put on the public record in the Senate by Senator Michael Baume[38].

. The timing of the Keating expose had everything to do with Packer firing a warning shot across the bows of the key men and women in the Coalition government, Howard, Costello and Alston and nothing to do with Keating's business failings.

Paul Keating commenting on the 60 Minutes expose of his piggery dealings[39] said, *"I think this is as much about demonstrating to the Prime Minister (John Howard) and his family where power resides as it is about trying to damage me."*

In 1994, Labor MP Chris Schacht said more bluntly:

"I suppose everyone is fearful that one day, if you told Kerry Packer to go jump, you might end up as a bad story in the newspapers. As a result, you might end up with an antagonistic

---

[38] http://www.gwb.com.au/gwb/news/onenation/keating/

[39] Page 11, Weekend Australian, 27/3/99

story. That's a natural function of human nature, I suppose. And no politician wants to see a bad story written about themselves, or against their government or their party."

The politicians have only themselves to blame. They have undermined our democracy by allowing such a concentrated media ownership.. media policy in this country is now effectively dictated by and in the interests of the Packer/Murdoch alliance.

The issues:

Today it is well nigh impossible to inform the Australian about matters in the public interest that are not in the interests of the Packer or Murdoch empires. The media has become a closed shop.

An example of this is the treatment meted out to my own book *"Murder by Media, Death of Democracy in Australia.*[40]*"* The book, which questions Australia's *"democracy"* and power through media control in Australia was sold by the large national Dymocks franchise for just three weeks before an extraordinary level of personal intervention by the chairman, John Forsyth.

Following the chairman's intervention the book was removed from sale by Dymocks with the managing director, Keith Perkin, writing the following in his explanation to the publishers, Interactive Presentations Pty Ltd:

I note your comment that the book cannot be the subject of legal threats because 'it is based on fact and what reporters have written over the last three years'. Even if that is in fact the case, we have been advised that truth alone is not a defence to defamation actions in Australia.

The irony that this book had been singled out and that hundreds of other books carried by the chain could well have fallen into the same category of defamation apparently failed to grasp Perkin.

"Murder by Media" was based on what newspapers had written and this appeared to be the basis of the Dymocks' decision. Clearly two sets of rules apply in Australia. Murdoch and Packer can publish and be damned while an Australian citizen reporting on extracts from their articles and opinion pieces can attract the attention of the courts in costly legal action.

The letter from Perkin carried a subtle but clear warning. It states,

I put you on notice that any statement which you make which suggests that Dymocks' decision resulted in any way from an

[40] http://www.gwb.com.au/murder.html

attempt to censor your book and the views expressed in it from being circulated, will result in the commencement of legal proceedings against you without notice.

The fact that John Forsyth, one of Australia's two hundred wealthiest individuals (worth about Au$200 million), is a close friend of Kerry Packer's should not go unreported.

The removal of the book from Dymocks went practically unreported. *The Courier-Mail* reported under the *Heading "Hanson book turmoil"*:

One of Australia's biggest bookstore chains has withdrawn a book about Pauline Hanson's botched federal election campaign from sale for legal reasons.

The book, "Murder by Media", was written by Hanson supporter and One Nation "webmaster" Scott Balson.

It had been on sale just one month before it was pulled from the shelves.

Dymocks board member John Millard yesterday said the matter was in the hands of Dymocks' legal advisers.

Mr Balson said he had received no complaints about the book.

The fact that the book is about media bias and not *"Hanson's botched federal election campaign"* reflects the media's callous disregard for the truth. No legal complaints have been received about the book's contents over three months after its launch.

One reporter, Paul Sheehan[41] from Fairfax's Sydney Morning Herald, did contact me shortly after its removal and advised that a story was going to be presented for publishing after *"legal clearance had been obtained"*.

Some weeks later Sheehan appeared to have lost interest saying that *"he was too busy"* – this despite his earlier comment during his initial contact when he said that *"he found it extraordinary that the media had not looked behind the withdrawal of the book"*.

It took the University of Queensland's Department of Journalism to question why in the March 1999 edition of The Queensland Independent in an article headed *"Study in media power an essential Australian text"*:[42]

Balson is the editor of the online newspaper, The Australian National News of the Day, in operation since October 1995. It is

---

[41] Sheehan – author of *"Amongst the Barbarians"*

[42] http://members.tripod.com/balson/uq2.htm

from this archive that much of the material in this book has been collated.

He has done this brilliantly. The level of research that has gone into producing this book is what makes it.

Far from crying wolf, Scott Balson has gone running through the village with photographs.

His views are supported, his assertions are researched, and so his attacks are grounded.

Surely, within any democracy, the powers that be need to be questioned, checked and challenged?

Surely, freedom of speech infers a right to speak freely?

In his research on media coverage of One Nation, Balson notes the numerous caricatures of Pauline Hanson featured in The Courier-Mail and it is interesting that an ordinary Australian who writes a book of some of his own opinions doesn't seem to be allowed the same degree of freedom?

What I have demonstrated above is a quite startling example of how clearly defined censorship in Australia is. The media barons are able to control what the people in Australia see, hear, and read. Through this control they are able to forge their own agenda to the detriment of the general population. Their willing and compliant partners are the major political parties who today depend on the goodwill of the media barons to survive.

As Senator Chris Schacht (Labor's Opposition Communications Spokesman) was reported as saying:

"He (Packer) and his organisation know how to play the political game, know how to lobby, know how to have influence and whenever there is something going that is in their interest, they, the Packer organisation, are pretty adept at making sure politicians of all sides know what the Packer interest is."

The journalists who do speak out about the growing monopoly in the media as the two media barons join forces do so at great risk to themselves and their careers. They face a life in the *"wilderness"*.

The standard of journalism is, no doubt, a casualty as more and more ethical reporters seeks careers outside the mainstream media or move overseas where their views can be expressed more freely. Many have taken to writing books or freelance work as they seek alternative employment opportunities.

The few ethical journalists that remain face a new threat represented by the media advisers of the major political parties. These faceless men and women are welcomed into papers around the country. From these positions they are able to compromise the ethics of good reporting by pushing the line of their own party.

The opinion writers used by the papers are today carefully selected – pushing the line that *"globalisation is good and unstoppable"* and that somehow the voice of the Australian people has no role to play in the forging of this country's future.

What the major parties think about media ownership:

The major political parties are totally beholden to the media barons. You will never see Prime Minister John Howard or the Minister for Communications, Senator Richard Alston, challenging or questioning media ownership in this country. To do so is political suicide. So entrenched is the high-level of political corruption that Liberal power broker Michael Kroger is *(like Labor's Graham Richardson was under Labor)* quite openly a middle man between Packer and key Liberal Senators like Communications Minister Senator Richard Alston.

The Labor party is no better, perhaps worse. Right now they have to curry favour with the media barons to regain government. Graham Richardson (ex-Labor Communication Minister) is one of Kerry Packer's paid advisers/power brokers.

In the 1980s Tom Burton (journalist and former government adviser) said[43]: *"There was a joke within the Cabinet that Graham Richardson was called the Minister for Channel 9. And between him and Peter Baron who was Bob Hawke's former senior adviser, they were very effective lobbyists. I remember quite clearly one day getting this piece of paper delivered from the Prime Minister's office, Bob Hawke's office, and we were told this is what Mr Hawke wants, well, and at the top of the page was a facsimile and it was from TCN9."*

In some areas of the media the cosy relationship between the major parties and the media barons is even more transparent.

For example, when Labor's Queensland state premier Wayne Goss lost government in 1996 the media advisers simply packed up their personal belongings and started work at Murdoch's *The Courier-Mail* newspaper as reporters the next day. The Murdoch press is full of ex-Labor and ex-Coalition media advisers. When Labor regained power in Queensland in June 1998 the soft-shoe shuffle from *The Courier-Mail* went, without question, in the other

---

[43] http://www.gwb.com.au/gwb/news/packer/packer1.html

direction with journalists becoming media advisers to their political master again. This is how the game is played, no rules and no questions are asked – this is far too close to home.

How the media have reported on this issue:

Forget it!

Is there a solution:

It is time for Australians to question why and what can be done to stop this sorry state of affairs continuing. It is not good enough to just sit at home and talk about it. Collective action is the only way to put pressure on the powers that be because they won't get the answers from today's politicians.

The most effective short term way of drawing attention to the bias of the media is through the Australian Press Council (APC). The APC handles media complaints on behalf of Australians. It has now made itself accessible to those on the Internet[44] where it states,

"The Australian Press Council is the self-regulatory body of the print media. It was established in 1976 with two main aims: to help preserve the traditional freedom of the press within Australia and ensure that the free press acts responsibly and ethically.."

For those with access to the Internet there is a simple process available to a complainant. This involves completing an on-line *"complaint form"*[45]. Before you do so it is important that you understand the APC's *"Statement of Principles"* – which are on-line[46]. The APC will respond to your complaint in writing requesting a copy of the offending article (remember to keep it). The APC contacts the editor of the paper publishing the article requesting an explanation. If the paper's explanation does not satisfy you (you are sent a copy of the reply) you are legitimately able to request the APC committee to arbitrate on your behalf. If the paper is found to be at fault they have to publish a retraction.

Here are some interesting statistics in relation to Australia's, until now, best kept secret[47] (only 434 complaints were registered with the APC in 1997/98):

---

44 http://www.presscouncil.org.au/pcsite/apc.html

45 http://www.presscouncil.org.au/pcsite/compform.html

46 http://www.presscouncil.org.au/pcsite/complaints/sop.html

47 http://www.gwb.com.au/gwb/news/99a/apc2.gif

Category of Complaint	No. Complaints 1988/97	No. Complaints 1997/98	'97/98 % of total complaint '88/97
Headline: false/misleading	93	47	*51% of total*
Sensationalism	54	10	19% of total
Bias	142	25	18% of total
Distortion	135	16	18% of total
Invasion of Privacy	170	29	17% of total
Racism	194	22	11% of total
Bad taste	53	2	4% of total
Sexism	81	3	4% of total

For those not on the Internet, contact the *Australian Press Council* on their toll free phone number: **1800 025712** and request them to send you a complaint form.

In the longer term, just as government policy has allowed the Packer and Murdoch families to take over control of Australia's media, policy can be changed to force them to sell their controlling interest in many of their media assets.

This of course makes perfect sense to the 99.9% of the Australian population outside the *"system"*. Unfortunately democracy doesn't work this way in Australia at the moment – not under the two party system where those in power now depend on the goodwill of the Packer/Murdoch duopoly for their very political survival.

The only way democracy can be returned to the Australian voter is through the ballot box. And the answer lies in a political party established outside the two party *"system"*.

The question is: *Do Australians care for their future enough to become politically active or is the nation bound for a future determined not by the people, for the people but by the media barons, for the media barons? And will the people, next time round, understand the role that this country's press plays in destroying political threats to the media masters.*

As long as the status quo in media concentration is allowed to remain the issues raised in this book will be pushed under the carpet.

These issues highlight the bias and self-interest of the Packer/Murdoch empires. These de-facto multinational companies are already benefiting enormously from globalisation and the resulting falling standards of living amongst Australians.

Further research:
http://www.gwb.com.au/gwb/news/four

Chapter 13
The Aboriginal Industry

Background:

This race-based organisation is a product of the referendum in 1967 which approved an amendment to the Australian constitution. This amendment had the primary and commendable aim of ensuring that all Australians (including specifically the indigenous people) had equal rights. However, the wording of the amendment singled out the indigenous race and created the legal loophole for race-baced industries to be born.

The Aboriginal Industry has already spawned a multitude of weird and wonderful racially-specific bureaucracies.

The grand-daddy of them all is known as the Aboriginal and Torres Strait Islander Commission (or ATSIC). ATSIC has been fed by tens of billions of dollars of tax payer funding over the years following its creation by the Australian federal government.

The biggest flaw with the ATSIC operation is its bureaucratic structure. When you tie this together with political correctness and the ability to hide behind the skirts of the Anti-Discrimination Commission and other minority-based bureaucracies you have a real problem. Any challenge against ATSIC, however credible, is immediately labelled a *"racist"* attack.

Very few of the billions of dollars that have been handed to ATSIC by Australian governments have ever reached their official destination. While ATSIC's primary aim was supposed to be the social upliftment of the indigenous people it has now degenerated into a financially driven bureaucracy out of touch with this primary goal. For example, a large percentage of the money is now used in the courts to fight expensive and drawn out native title claims and to take race-based issues through the courts – right up to the High Court. Money is no object much to the delight of the legal profession feeding off ATSIC like vultures around a kill.

In reality ATSIC has evolved into a bureaucratic beast which feeds off fear and intimidation.

Tragically, the indigenous people who really need the funding that ATSIC control rarely, if ever, get to see the fruits of the tax payer's generosity. These disadvantaged Aboriginals and Torres Strait Islanders are often left to tend for themselves in remote areas under third world conditions. When these conditions are exposed the media and ATSIC councillors or bureaucrats point the finger at the government putting further pressure on them under the mantle of *"racism"*. Australia has now been singled out in the developed world by the UN for its poor treatment of its indigenous people.

ATSIC has also been the backbone behind a number of divisive and race-based reports, inquiries and investigations such as:

- **The "Bringing them home" taskforce**

This inquiry was established to investigate claims that Aboriginal children had been *"stolen"* from their parents in the 1950s so that they could be brought up with a *"whiteman's"* education. Unsurprisingly the report was co-ordinated by the Human Rights and Equal Opportunities Commission (HREOC)

In its submission to the inquiry ATSIC demanded that

...increased Government funding be provided to Aboriginal and Torres Strait Islander organisations to establish and support appropriate mental health services for indigenous people, with a particular emphasis on the provision of services to those who experienced childhood separation.

...the Inquiry make recommendations to Government on suitable options for compensation recognising the need for a diversity of mechanisms to address the different needs of those who have been subjected to separation policies.

...governments and relevant non-government agencies acknowledge that separation policies were unjust and apologise to all indigenous Australians for the harms to indigenous communities, families and individuals.

Apparently the billions of dollars already being consumed by the Aboriginal industry are not enough – and each and every cause that ATSIC now embraces, on legally designed grounds, has a financial bottom line as its basis.

The reality of what happened to the *"stolen children"* was vastly different from the resulting politically correct report produced by Sir Ronald Wilson, former justice of the High Court, President of the Uniting Church of Australia and Human Rights and Equal Opportunities Commissioner.

During the period under investigation by Wilson half-caste kids would now and again turn up at missions with spear marks and signs of horrific beltings. Babies were occasionally abandoned and young children left to fend for themselves. *"Yella fellas"* could find themselves in no-mans-land.

Most of these children were rescued by welfare officers. They were not stolen.

On March 9th 1999 Lawrie Kavanagh reported in *The Courier-Mail* in an article headed *"Stolen children policy more a rescue mission"*,

"This included his (Dr Walter Roth's) experiences of Aboriginal infanticide which alerted him to the grim fate hanging over some children, particularly half-caste children."

"... it is not difficult to believe what author Colin Macleod wrote about the no-win situation into which half-castes were born. Whitefellas intervened and now stand condemned.

"The rescue operation mounted by such people as Macleod is now branded as genocide by those who would re-write history for whatever reason."

Despite these facts the *"Bringing them Home"* report made the most outrageous finding that the policies of removing Aboriginal children to save them and to assimilate them into the broader Australian society constituted *"genocide"* under the United Nations Genocide Convention because the policy was designed to destroy Aboriginal *"cultural units"*.

There are ATSIC funded test cases resulting from the report currently before the courts. These test cases, sympathetically reported on by the media, have financial compensation as the backbone of their instigation. The Commonwealth of Australia, which has been aggressively defending the action, discovered through investigations that the complainants were *"rescued"* by those caring from them.

Ironically many of the most outspoken Aboriginals of today have their *"stolen generation"* upbringing to thank for their high level of education and ability to now use *"whiteman's law"* against ***him***.

There are a growing number of unreported, little-known bodies which have sprung up through ATSIC. Once again the common theme behind them appears to be a financial/legalistic bent not a social interest. Examples include the findings of the:

- **"Building on Land Rights for the next generation" report.**

This report by ATSIC covers the Aboriginal *"ownership"* of lands in the Northern Territory.

In the reports findings ATSIC state:

Easily the most important social, cultural and economic outcome arising from the transfer of 573 000 km^2—42.3 per cent of the Northern Territory to Aboriginal Territorians is the huge *consumption gain that has accrued to them as a result. Since much of the land claimed is of marginal economic value in alternative uses creating a situation that enables Aboriginal Territorians to own, live on or freely visit their traditional 'countries' is a highly productive use of this land.*

The report talks about the *"Aboriginal Benefits Reserve"* (ABR) which reflects just one of many revenue bases being developed under ATSIC. Revenue bases which are over and above the billions of dollars of dollars of tax payers money being spent on propping up ATSIC.

It complains in legalistic terminology that: *The mining royalty equivalent payments made to the ABR from the Consolidated Revenue Fund are 'public' monies paid pursuant to a public policy decision of the Government. The recipients of these monies are accountable for them as public monies. The Royalty Associations should have been required to give an account of the expenditure of these monies pursuant to the same regulatory regime under which the Land Councils and ATSIC were working.*

It continues hypocritically[48], *For these reasons, the Royalty Associations have not been required to give a proper account of their expenditure of the 'areas affected' monies and it is doubtful whether those monies have been applied to their intended purposes. It is probable that a large part of those monies have been distributed in payments to individuals unrelated to a purpose. Such payments will only increase the dependence of Aboriginal Territorians on unearned income and prevent an accumulation of those monies for the long-term benefit of Aboriginal Territorians.*

Unlike the ABR the Indigenous Land Corporation[49] (ILC) is a taxpayer funded body that no-one hears very much about - but it has done very nicely since its establishment under the Labor government in 1995.

The Land Fund (administered by the ILC) was allocated Au$200 million in its first year and thereafter an allocation of Au$121 Million per year until 2004 – or a total of Au$1.289 Billion. The yearly allocation was indexed from 1996 to maintain the value in 1996 dollar terms. Of this Au$121 million allocated each year, Au$76 million is retained in the Land Fund, Au$45 million goes to

---

[48] Consider the lack of records of spending kept by many ATSIC Councils.

[49] http://www.ilc.gov.au/

the ILC for land acquisition and management. The ILC is already the largest single land owner in Australia.

We often see those who have held senior positions in ATSIC gaining major financial benefit from their association with the body. There is, perhaps, no better example of this than ex-ATSIC councillor Charlie Perkins. Perkins, today a millionaire with a splendid home in Sydney, is widely in the Aboriginal community as "Mr 5%" because of the cut that he demanded from Aboriginal native title claimants and those on the other side of the claim when it came to settlements that he *"negotiated"*.

Today Perkins is often seen on television or heard on radio tearing strips off anyone who dare speak out about or questioning ATSIC. His colourful language includes claims that these people are *"racists, bigots and red-necks"*.

ATSIC Councillors are extremely well paid, are treated like kings and can do no wrong. Prominent Aborigines and ATSIC councillors like Noel Pearson, Geoff Clark and Michael Neal now act as consultants to legal firms on *"native title issues"*. It appears that the relationship is a financial win-win for both sides of this arrangement.

It is through these types of backroom associations and funded groups that billions of dollars of ATSIC funding is now being filtered from supporting those most in need to those who are making a financial killing through the growing native title industry.

Finally, despite claims that ATSIC has now been audited the results of reports released to date show massive misuse of the tax payer funds provided to bodies accountable to it. The media's reporting on these reports has been clouded and shrouded under a grey area of political correctness and claims by those being singled out in the reports that their findings are, once again, *"racist"*.

The issues:

First, consider the amount of time, money and energy which is being spent and dedicated to issues like the politically correct *"Bringing them Home"* report and native title. Is it not then palpably irresponsible, perhaps bordering on the most extreme degree of neglect that the **real issues** like *"globalisation"* – especially in clearly identified areas like the MAI and the FSIA are not being debated in great depth on the same basis in the media or in parliament?

The Aboriginal Industry

The manner in which money is being diverted from its primary aim of supporting those Aborigines most in need to lawyers bank accounts is an issue which has never received the attention that it really deserves. The idea that the indigenous population should have the freedom to determine their own future through bodies like ATSIC is destroyed when one considers the abysmal track record of this *"indigenous"* industry.

Meanwhile, the country's sovereignty is apparently not worth public consideration while divisive, race based issues revolving around ATSIC and native title attract the highest degree of input from think tanks and legal minds in Australia.

What the major parties think about this issue:

ATSIC is a political hot potato given life by the Labor party. Both the major parties, as in the case of the multicultural industry, prefer to steer a wide berth around the corruption that is openly taking place within the organisation.

The Labor Party have been particularly close to the Aboriginal industry. A classic example of this is the Hindmarsh Island case in which a story was concocted by a couple of women in the Ngarrindjeri tribe which was swallowed as fact by none other than then Labor Minister for Aboriginal Affairs Robert Tickner and the Labor cabinet. The case blew up in 1995 when the Tom and Wendy Chapman were taken to court over the proposed building of a bridge between the mainland and Hindmarsh Island near Adelaide.

As a result of the action by the women the Chapman's company developing the bridge was put into bankruptcy by Westpac. At the time the mainstream media treated the case, in the main, with a one-eyed perspective in which the Chapman's were the villains and the Aboriginal claimants were the victims. The reverse was later proven to be the case. Books by Chris Kenny *"It would be nice if there was some secret women's business"* (Duffy & Snellgrove, 1996) and by a member of the Ngarrindjeri tribe, Dulcie Wilson, *"The cost of crossing bridges"* (Small Poppies Publishing, Melbourne, 1998) reveal the real story on this fraudulent claim that would never otherwise have been fully exposed.

It was only many years later because of the protective guise put by ATSIC's lawyers of *"secret women's business"* that the truth came out. The laughable case put forward by the claimants was that Hindmarsh Island had some spiritual significance because it looked like *"a woman's private parts"* when seen from the air. The story was apparently hatched after the claimants saw an aerial photograph of Hindmarsh and the *"woman's business"* claim was hatched.

Of course you don't have to be an Einstein to realise that the traditional Aborigines could not have seen the island from the air – making their case a complete and utter scandalous joke. Somehow the Australians courts could not immediately recognise the rather strange basis of the claim.

The silence that both the media and the major parties have greeted this ATSIC contrived travesty against the Chapman's (white Australian citizens), in itself, speaks more loudly than any front page headline in the papers.

How the media have reported on this issue:

The media hardly questioned the **"Bringing them Home"** report despite the people who drafted it claiming that the plight of young Aborigines and their nation as victims of genocide under the genocide convention.

ATSIC and its numerous off-shoots are rarely, if ever, questioned by the media despite plenty of ammunition for them to do so.

The real victims of the Hindmarsh Island fiasco, Mr and Mrs Chapman, are currently winning a number of defamation cases against the mainstream media and politically correct publications which denigrated them without reason. The wins reveal the politically correct nature of biased articles aimed at undermining their fight against the fraudulent claim made by a couple of Ngarrindjeri women, financially backed through the courts by ATSIC funds through the Aboriginal Legal Rights Movement.

Unfortunately the manner in which the Chapman's were treated by the media cannot be seen in isolation. The victimisation by the media of anyone challenging the Aboriginal industry can be taken as fate accompli.

Is there a solution:

Organisations like ATSIC and the ILC should be disbanded and absorbed back into services provided by the mainstream Australian population.

The identification of bodies by race is, in itself, divisive and an act of racism that Australia cannot afford to support at either a financial or social level.

Chapter 14
Native Title And Beyond

Background:

Pre the High Court's decision on Wik pastoralists and miners believed that they held title over property through their leasehold.

The change started when on 30 June 1993 (before the *Native Title Act* became law in December 1993) the Wik Peoples made a claim for native title in the Federal Court of Australia to land on Cape York Peninsula in Queensland.

The Thayorre People, funded by the Aboriginal Legal Service, joined the action, claiming native title rights to an area partly overlapping the Wik Peoples' claim. The land claimed by the Wik Peoples and the Thayorre People included land where two pastoral leases were granted by the Queensland Government.

One pastoral lease of 1119 square miles (2830 square kms), originally granted in 1945, continues to be a pastoral lease. The current lease was granted in 1975 and expires in the year 2004. It has never been permanently occupied or fenced. In 1988 it was reported that it carried only 100 unbranded cattle.

The other pastoral lease was 535 square miles (1385 square kms). It was first granted in 1915. It was forfeited and replaced by another pastoral lease in 1919 and forfeited again in 1920. In fact, it was never occupied as a pastoral lease. Aboriginal people, however, have been in continuous occupation of that area. About 300 were recorded as being present in 1919. In 1922 the area became an Aboriginal Reserve and remains so today.

The Wik Peoples and the Thayorre People argued that native title co-existed with the pastoral leases.

On 29 January 1996, Justice Drummond in the Federal Court made a decision that the claim of the Wik and Thayorre Peoples could not succeed over the areas as they were subject to pastoral leases. The Judge's reason was that he considered that the grant of pastoral leases under Queensland law extinguished any native title rights.

The judges findings were in line with the agreement struck between Aboriginal elders and government under Paul Keating that *"pastoral leases were not subject to native title claims"*.

The Wik People were not satisfied with the ruling so they went to the High Court to appeal that decision. The Appeal was highly legalistic and specifically targeted against answers which Justice Drummond had given to several legal questions. It was aimed at opening up the question of native title over pastoral leases. A money tree to the legal profession depending on the decision.

The most important of the questions presented related to the two pastoral leases. The question asked in the case of each pastoral lease was:

"Does the pastoral lease confer rights to exclusive possession on the grantee [ie. the pastoralist]?"

The High Court did not make a decision in the Wik Case about what native title rights the Wik Peoples or the Thayorre People had. Neither did the High Court decide on the actual native title rights of the Wik and Thayorre Peoples because of the manner in which the case got to the High Court. It was an appeal against a decision made by Justice Drummond who made his ruling before hearing any of the evidence of the Wik Peoples' claim to native title.

The High Court said that Drummond was wrong on these questions and that the Wik Peoples should be able to go back to the Federal Court and present evidence to prove their native title rights thus opening the legal loophole over pastoral leases.

The High Court, in the Mabo case, said that native title rights must be proved by evidence of the customs and traditions of the native title claimants. Those customs and *traditions may be different* in parts of Australia.

The Federal Court could now decide what the native title rights of the Wik Peoples were and which of those rights could co-exist with the pastoral lease. Alternatively, the Queensland Government would now be forced to sit down with the Aboriginal people and negotiate an agreement using the procedures of the *Native Title Act.* In theory such an agreement would recognise the rights of everybody, thus avoiding expensive litigation. In reality the legal costs being paid for by ATSIC (on behalf of the claimants) and the leaseholder respondents like farmers (legal costs funded personally) when unsuccessful claims were taken to a higher court.

The High Court said that the only native title rights that could co-exist with the rights of a pastoralist holding a lease are *those that are not inconsistent with the rights of the pastoralist.* However, if an agreement cannot be reached between the parties then the High Court said the Federal Court could make a final determination on native title and compare the native title rights with the rights

under the pastoral lease. It may be, for example, rule that rights to visit sacred sites, hold ceremonies and collect native foods would not be seen as inconsistent with the pastoralists' rights.
These new native title rights ruled that a native title holder:

- could not exclude the holder of a pastoral lease from the area of the pastoral lease or restrict pastoralists from using the lease area for pastoral purposes.
- could not, therefore, have full beneficial ownership of the land at the same time as it is the subject of a pastoral lease.
- would not be able to do anything which interfered with:
- the ability of the pastoralist's livestock to take advantage of the pasture and water sources on the land;
- the pastoralist's privacy on the homestead and
- the pastoralist's right to build fences, gates, windmills and other improvements to the land.

The High Court made it very clear that none of the *existing* rights of the pastoral leases should be taken away by co-existing native title rights. Where there is any inconsistency with a pastoralist's rights, the pastoralist's rights would override native title. However, the can of worms was opened when it came to the lease holder wanting to develop his property in areas in which states would traditionally have had a say.

The High Court in the Wik Case confirmed its view in the Mabo Case that Governments have power to grant valid pastoral leases. The *Native Title Act 1993* validated any grants of pastoral leases which might have been invalid because of native title.

The High Court overrode the *Native Title Act of 1993* when its Wik ruling confirmed that a pastoral lease gave the pastoralist the right to use the land for pastoral purposes but setting out what the lease *"limitations"* were.

The High Court said that pastoral purposes would include:

- raising livestock;
- establishing fences, yards, bores, mills and accommodation.

The High Court further established that a pastoral lessee's rights would be defined by the relevant State Statute. An example of a relevant State Statute is the *Land Act* of WA. It gives a pastoral lessee the natural surface of the land for pastoral purposes. It does not give general rights to soil or timber but gives specific rights to:

- take soil and timber for domestic purposes;

- take soil and timber for the construction of airstrips, roads, buildings, fences, stockyards or other improvements on the land;
- sow and cultivate non-indigenous pasture species with the approval of the State Minister.

This was a major shift from the understanding of the *Native Title Act of 1993* – quickly leading to over 80% of Australia being claimed under native title and a financial windfall for lawyers.

For example, the High Court pointed out that pastoral leases in Queensland are subject to statutory provisions which define the right of a pastoralist, (as they are in the other parts of Australia) including conditions:

- requiring that the land be developed, improved or enclosed by fencing;
- requiring the destruction of noxious plants and the control of vermin;
- prohibiting the destruction of trees;
- making leases subject to rights granted under mining legislation, petroleum legislation and forestry legislation;
- keeping for the Government the power to allow other persons to enter the land to take soil or timber or for "any purpose";
- giving drovers and others the right to pass through pastoral leases and use pastures while passing through.

These provisions are generally limited by the Statute to protect the privacy of the homestead and gardens and paddocks under cultivation.

In other States such as Western Australia, South Australia and the Northern Territory, Statutes provide that Aboriginal people have a right to enter pastoral leases in order to live off the land in their traditional manner. Those provisions also have limitations which protect improved parts of properties.

Some statutory provisions stop pastoralists carrying out certain activities on pastoral leases except with State Government approval.

This is where the conflict arises under the Wik decision arises.

If the Government's approval is required for a certain act where native title co-exists, ***(like building a dam)*** the Government and the lessee need to take into account the *Native Title Act 1993* before approval can be given. The extent to which any provisions of the Act apply will require further investigation.

Pastoralists' rights under their leases have changed as a result of the Wik decision, but they retain the same legal interest as was their legal entitlement prior to the decision because the native title holders can now prevent them developing the property.

Despite this ATSIC claim that there is no legal impact on:

- the value of the pastoral lease
- the value of the security which the pastoral lease may provide for borrowing money.

ATSIC claim that financial institutions base their valuations of pastoral leases for security for a loan on its capacity to carry stock (and hence its ability to generate income), the equipment owned by the pastoralist and improvements (houses, fences, dams, yards etc). The organisation says that all these things are unaffected by the Wik decision. Typically, a pastoralist would use the livestock on the land as security for a loan. This is known as a stock mortgage. Again, these arrangements are unaffected by the Wik decision.

However the banks do not see this issue so black and white with threats that loans provided to farms would be re-evaluated if native title claims were made over them. The banks' case is understandable – the pastoralist now has to gain agreement from *"native title holders"* if it wants to build a dam to support increased numbers of cattle or for irrigating crops.

There are no compensation obligations on pastoralists flowing from the Wik decision. Any compensation payable to pastoralists because of the prevention or impairment of a proposed development (like a dam) is payable by the Government which made the law requiring approval. This, however, requires more costly legal argument – something farmers today cannot afford.

Since the commencement of the *Native Title Act* on 1st January 1994 the grant of all mining tenements over land where native title may still exist has to go through a right to negotiate process. This involves governments notifying native title holders of its intention to grant the mining tenement, allowing the native title holders a short time to register their claim and, if it is registered, negotiations between the native title holders, the mining company and the Government. If no agreement can be reached, then the National Native Title Tribunal or a similar State body decides if exploration or mining can go ahead and on what conditions.

There are also mechanisms in the *Native Title Act* to avoid or fast track the right to negotiate process in some circumstances.

All grants of mining tenements on pastoral leases since 1st January 1994 should have gone through the right to negotiate process as the question of the continued existence of native title on pastoral leases was not resolved by the Mabo case or the *Native Title Act*. In finding that some native title rights may coexist with pastoral leases the Wik case, extraordinarily, confirmed the need for government to use the right to negotiate process on these leases.

If native title claims are made over pastoral leases upon which mining tenements existed prior to the *Native Title Act*, the native title rights are subject to the rights of miners to continue mining. In those instances, the right to negotiate process under the Act will not apply.

However, if a government granted mining tenements on pastoral leases after the *Native Title Act* without going through the right to negotiate process, those mining tenements could prove to be invalid!

Fr Cyril Connolly MSC[50], informed by tribal elders from the Top End *(tribal law elders being the only appropriate source of information of this nature)* offers the following principles of customary tribal law with respect to succession to tribal land:

- tribal customary law recognises native title rights to reside only in those persons who are aboriginal by their law. This means that a person must be born of a tribally initiated father and mother and no one else.
- Native Title rights are vested only in the male person. His authority over his land or *"country"* increases as he progresses through the levels of ceremonial law. Here again no one is admitted to the process of ceremonial law and its rituals unless he qualifies by being born of a tribal father and mother.
- Native Title to land does not reside in the woman, nor does it descend, in tribal customary law, through the female line.
- there is no provision in customary tribal law for making someone into an aboriginal by defining them to be one.
- a person who has a non-custodial father and a tribal mother has visiting rights to his mother's country and can stay there. He

[50] http://www.gwb.com.au/gwb/news/onenation/title/priest.html

may also take part in some of the discussions but he has no land 'ownership' rights; no native title rights.

By allowing mixed-race aborigines to participate as native title claimants, the Native Title Act adapts its own version of tribal customary law and, in so doing, strays from the test of the High Court under the original Mabo decision that native title must be ascertained in accordance with "their" laws and customs.

Thus, whilst the High Court has said that native title still exists in Australia, the fact that there will be no existing eligible native title claimant unless traditional native law with respect to such claimant is satisfied has become a politically correct casualty under the law.

Mixed-race aborigines are not legitimate native title claimants and the Native Title Act should be amended to clearly reflect the fact that as native title claims, under Mabo, are based on Aboriginal tribal law. It doesn't, even though native title claims by mixed-race and female aborigines is inherently unjust.

Nothing, however, gets in the way of political correctness.

Because of the complete and utter confusion following the High Court's controversial decision on Wik, the Coalition government brought out its own ten point plan on Wik.

The points being:

1: Validation of acts/grants between 1/1/94 and 23/12/96

Legislative action will be taken to ensure that the validity of any acts or grants made in relation to non-vacant crown land in the period between passage of the Native Title Act (NTA) and the Wik decision is put beyond doubt.

2: Confirmation of extinguishment of native title on "exclusive" tenures.

States and Territories would be able to confirm that "exclusive" tenures such as freehold, residential, commercial and public works in existence on or before 1 January 1994 extinguish native title. Agricultural leases would also be covered to the extent that it can reasonably be said that by reason of the grant or the nature of the permitted use of the land, exclusive possession must have been intended. Any current or former pastoral lease conferring exclusive possession would also be included.

3: Provision of Services

Impediments to the provision of government services in relation to land on which native title may exist would be removed.

4: Native title and pastoral leases

As provided in the Wik decision, native title rights over current or former pastoral leases and any agricultural leases not covered under 2 above would be permanently extinguished to the extent that those rights are inconsistent with those of the pastoralist. All activities pursuant to, or incidental to, "primary production" (this will be based on the definition in the Income Tax Assessment Act 1936) would be allowed on pastoral leases including farmstay tourism, even if native title exists, provided the dominant purpose of the use of the land is primary production. However, future government action such as upgrading of title to perpetual or "exclusive" leases or freehold, would necessitate the acquisition of any native title rights proven to exist and the application of the regime described in 7 below (except where this is unnecessary because the pastoralist has an existing legally enforceable right to upgrade).

5: Statutory access rights

Where registered claimants can demonstrate that they currently have physical access to pastoral lease land, their continued access will be legislatively confirmed until the native title claim is determined. This would not affect existing access rights established by state or territory legislation.

6: Future mining activity

For mining on vacant crown land there would be a higher registration test for claimants seeking the right to negotiate, no negotiations on exploration, and only one right to negotiate per project. As currently provided in the NTA, states and territories would be able to put in place alternative regimes with similar right to negotiate provisions. For mining on other "non-exclusive" tenures such as current or former pastoral leasehold land and national parks, the right to negotiate would continue to apply in a state or territory unless and until that state or territory provided a statutory regime acceptable to the Commonwealth which included procedural rights at least equivalent to other parties with an interest in the land (eg the holder of the pastoral lease) and compensation which can take account of the nature of co-existing native title rights (where they are proven to exist).

7: Future government and commercial development

On vacant crown land outside towns and cities there would be a higher registration test to access the right to negotiate, but the right to negotiate would be removed in relation to the acquisition of native title rights for third parties for the purpose of government-type infrastructure. As currently provided in the NTA, states and territories would be able to put in place alternative regimes with similar right to negotiate provisions. For compulsory acquisition of native title rights on other "non-exclusive" tenures such as current or former pastoral leasehold land and national parks, the right to negotiate would continue to apply in a state or territory unless and until that state or territory provided a statutory regime acceptable to the Commonwealth which included procedural rights at least equivalent to other parties with an interest in the land (eg the holder of the pastoral lease) and compensation which can take account of co-existing native title rights (where they are proven to exist). The right to negotiate would be removed in relation to the acquisition of land for third parties in towns and cities, although native title holders would gain the same procedural and compensation rights as other landholders. Future actions for the management of any existing national park or forest reserve would be allowed. A regime to authorise activities such as the taking of timber or gravel on pastoral leases would be provided.

8: Management of water resources and airspace

The ability of governments to regulate and manage surface and subsurface water, off-shore resources and airspace, and the rights of those with interests under any such regulatory or management regime would be put beyond doubt.

9: Management of claims

In relation to new and existing native title claims, there would be a higher registration test to access the right to negotiate, amendments to speed up handling of claims, and measures to encourage the states to manage claims within their own systems. A sunset clause within which new claims would have to be made would be introduced.

10: Agreements

Measures would be introduced to facilitate the negotiation of voluntary but binding agreements as an alternative to more formal native title machinery.

Each state has been given a free hand to adopt all or parts of the ten point plan creating a legal nightmare.

The real frightening outcome of native title can be found in the current *"Draft Declaration on the Rights of Indigenous People"* – underwriting race based autonomy.

Native Title And Beyond

In June 1998 Ms Hanson used Parliament to raise the possibility of native title, through the UN negotiations, leading to Nunavut-type autonomy claims. Nunavut is a new Inuit (Eskimo) state in northern Canada taking up 20% of that country's land mass.

John Howard responded to Ms Hanson's comments on Radio National a few days later saying, *"Well I read the speech that she made last night and I've got to say that it is not only an inaccurate dishonest speech but it verges on the deranged in various places...*

"What she said in this statement is appealing to irresponsible, racist sentiment in the community."

Then less than a year later, in March 1999, it was reported that Torres Strait Islander leaders met with Prime Minister John Howard and Queensland State Premier Peter Beattie to discuss *"autonomy"* - with self government along the lines of Norfolk Island – or Nunavut.

A proposal was submitted for the establishment of a Torres Strait Regional Assembly 2001 - giving the region *territory status.* When this happens the fragmenting of Australia on racial lines will have begun.

A spokesman for Howard's office said at this time that the *Coalition had made an election commitment to grant autonomy to the Torres Strait Region.* ***"And the government is continuing dialogue to that end."***

This, just nine months after Prime Minister John Howard had called Ms Hanson *"deranged"* for suggesting what was obviously already being negotiated by his office behind closed doors.

The leader of the autonomy group, John Abendigo told reporters before his meeting with the Queensland Premier, *"This does not mean that we break away from Australia - we're still part of Australia because we want to remain part of Australia.*

"This is our first meeting with the Premier (Peter Beattie) since he came into office, so we're going to use this meeting to gauge his support.

"At the autonomy meeting we had a good representation of a cross-section of people living in the region and it was apparent that there is support for the concept of autonomy right across the Torres Strait."

What appears to be lost to everybody involved in this debate is the following:

- Torres Strait is most vulnerable to Indonesian aggression - and a useful foothold into Australia.

- Australians (like Canadians in the case of Nunavut) will be footing the new territory's bills - thus the comment *"we want to remain part of Australia"*.

The issues:

Native title is nothing more than a legal nightmare. It has been latched onto by large legal firms which spunge off political correctness. It is fracturing and weakening Australia – a ploy which plays into the hands of the globalists and the world government.

The victims of native title are not the indigenous people but hundreds of thousands of family farmers who often find that they are defending multiple native title claims on their properties. While the Aboriginal claimants get unlimited access to funding for legal aid the farmers have to fund their own defence.

The longer term outlook for this debacle is autonomy and race based division – a horrifying thought which Australia is steadily lurching towards under the mantle of political correctness.

Native title is now being protected by the International Courts with the *UN Draft Declaration on the Rights of Indigenous Peoples* being another spoke in the wheel of globalism as Australia is fractured into race based states.

What the major parties think about this issue:

The Labor Party support native title and have, in cases like Hindmarsh Island, played an active part in pushing the case for the Aboriginal claimants. The Hindmarsh Island fiasco classically highlights the travesty of native title and political intervention.

Labor policy on native title states, *Native title rights are legal property rights, fully entitled to the same respect and protection as the property rights of other citizens. Legislative extinguishment of those rights, as they now co-exist on pastoral leases, whether direct or de facto, would necessarily be discriminatory and is unacceptable on moral, legal and financial grounds.*

The Coalition (largely through the demands of the National Party) have taken a firmer stand on native title. They are unhappy with the controversial High Court decision on Wik resulting in the tabling of the *"Ten Point Plan"*.

The National Party, in the lead up to the 1998 elections found it politically expedient to claim that they were taking a tough stand on Native Title, but once again their largely rural electorate were to be let down when the Coalition supported *"Indigenous autonomy"*

– or self-rule along racial lines. This is a dramatic shift in direction from 1988 when John Howard referred to a proposed treaty with the indigenous people as "a treaty for separatism".

Under the heading *"One Australia"* Howard wrote:

While a treaty may give some people a warm inner glow of satisfaction, it cannot and will not result in the development of compassionate and sensible policies so separately needed to overcome the situation faced by many Aboriginal people. On a recent visit to Alice Springs I met the chairman of the Central Lands Council, Wenten Rabuntja. In the course of our conversation he said that 'we are all one mob but some of us have bigger problems than others'. This to me, epitomises my ideal of One Australia and the way we should work together to overcome all areas of real disadvantage and not focus on the things that divide us, separate us and lead to a lack of understanding.

I regard a treaty as a recipe for separatism. I believe that those Aboriginal people who have served on the Australian Armed forces are proud of their achievements and would be insulted with the notion of having to turn around, like an alien people, an sign a treaty with their former comrades.

As I do not believe that a treaty is something that would be widely accepted I have no great fears that it will continue to be an issue of debate unless the Hawke Government decides for political reasons to continue with it. I hope this will not be the case as it can be to no Australian's advantage.

How the media have reported on this issue:

The media support native title claims. As mentioned earlier, in the Hindmarsh Island case, the Chapman's are now suing a number of mainstream publications for defamatory comments made at the height of the controversy over this native title claim.

A weakened and divided Australia is far easier to undermine than a people working together against the globalists. Native title is a key tool of division.

Is there a solution:

There is a simple solution to the native title problem. Native title should be extinguished through legislation in parliament and Australia must halt all negotiations with the UN on issues relating to native title and race-based agreements.

Chapter 15
Tax And Big Business

> *"The old pro-slaver serpent, beaten in the South, crawled up North and put on anti-slavery clothes and established his headquarters in Wall Street."*
> Congressman Alexander Campbell

Background:

The shifting of the tax burden from the rich onto the poor is the product of an unworkable tax system floundering under 30,000 pages of legislation and contradictory amendments to that legislation. Under Australian tax laws Australia's richest man Kerry Packer ***paid just Au$32.40 in tax over a three year period (about three cents a day)***. Kerry Packer, the person, is conservatively estimated to be worth over Au$5 billion. A battling pay-as-you-earn tax payer in Australia pays more tax in one week than Packer personally paid in three years.

Packer represents an extreme case of greed. According to the latest Australian Tax Office (ATO) figures people with a taxable income of more than Au$2 million a year paid just 21.3% in net tax. This compares with 24.7% for those in the Au$38,000 to Au$40,000 bracket (the average weekly male earnings). Those on Au$80,000 to Au$90,000 a year paid an average rate of net tax of 32.8% while those on Au$1 million to Au$2 million paid just 28.9%.

How can this be so?

The wheels started coming off when Paul Keating was treasurer. Keating was a friend of big business not the battler when he:

- cut 13 cents in the dollar off the top marginal rate of tax applying when John Howard was Treasurer in the pre-1983 Fraser Coalition government.
- introduced the dividend imputation system which slashed the amount of tax paid on income from shares.

When you add these tax breaks to the complex tax laws and the use of tax avoidance schemes through entities like trusts[51] and off-shore companies you soon realise how the mega-rich easily get around paying their fair share of the tax burden.

---

[51] The number of trusts has risen by 39.7% in the last five years.

Tax And Big Business

There are two outcomes from this debilitating but politically accepted travesty of balance.

- The first is that those who can least afford it have to make up the tax shortfall left by those avoiding tax.
- The second is that government services are adversely effected by the reduction in tax income.

Attached to this travesty is the fact that the services first feeling the financial pinch are those providing support to the growing underclass of poverty-stricken Australians. These are the Australians who will be most effected by the new tax, the GST (goods and services tax), creating an even wider gap between the rich and the poor in this country.

It has got to be understood that Kerry Packer, the person and the multinational, is not alone in playing tax avoidance to the nth degree. Overseas based multinationals, aside from Packer, have been buying up the Australian farm while using a number of *"legitimate"* tax avoidance schemes to maximise profits. Schemes commonly used include off-shore tax havens and international transfer pricing arrangements to minimise tax paid to the Australian government on profits made here from business transacted in this country. The financial cycle of rape and possession is complete.

On the 3rd April 1998 the ATO's Killaly said on ABC radio:

"There are 4,300 ***large*** *foreign corporations that pay no tax in Australia, and there are another 4,000 or so foreign companies that pay little or no tax in Australia by means of transfer pricing and various tax havens."*

It is a fact that 58% of the nation's 560,000 companies paid zero tax in 1996/7. The figure comes from the ATO and is a dramatic rise from the 53.3% paying no tax in 1994/5. Another 54,000 paid less than Au$1,000 in 1996/7. To top this the wealthy shareholders now get their dividends tax free. Kerry Packer, for example, was able to use Keating's dividend imputation system to receive about Au$600 million last year tax free from his dividends in his publicly listed company, Publishing and Broadcasting Ltd. Despite this he still had a go at the ex-Prime Minister and his bodgie piggery dealings to push a point to Howard over media ownership.

The tax avoidance schemes used by wealthy families has become an expedient political football in the past.

The Sydney Morning Herald wrote on the 17th September 1997:

Tax And Big Business

One of the advisers to many of the 100 families on this hit-list, the Melbourne-based lawyer Mark Leibler, detailed the embarrassing backdown by the ATO, Treasury and the Howard Government in a paper to a conference in June on "Effective Utilisation of Trust Structures". Leibler describes the crackdown as a "witch hunt", and defends the legitimate use of trusts.

In May last year, Costello began the back-pedalling when he announced that collection of the $800million had been deferred by one year "to allow time to develop appropriate responses to extremely complex issues".

Costello's August Budget said that the figure was merely the amount of "revenue at risk", rather than what could be collected. Instead of $800million, the Budget papers put an estimate of $100million for this financial year and said it was impossible to make estimates for subsequent years.

This assessment was quite at odds with Ralph Willis' announcement of the crackdown, which talked about "additional revenue" of $800million.

The residual is a mere estimate of the amount of revenue lost from tax minimisation by these 100 families. Collecting the money, as experience has shown, is another thing altogether.

The whole exercise by companies and extremely wealthy individuals as outlined above can be compared to the financial raping and pillaging of a city by a foreign force. In this case the foreign force are the wealthy tax avoiders and the inhabitants are the Australian tax payers. The rapidly deteriorating state of the buildings in the *"city"* are the people's living standards.

Another area of dubious taxation reform can be found in changes flagged for Capital Gains. About 80% of the capital gains tax paid by individuals in 1996-97 was paid by those on more than Au$50,000 a year while only 6% of those in the Au$20,700 to Au$38,000 income range paid this tax.

If Treasurer Peter Costello goes ahead with his plan to exempt the first Au$1,000 in capital gains from tax, the main beneficiaries will be those on the top income brackets. John Ralph, the head of Costello's company tax committee has warned that *the exemption invites tax avoidance only by those able to split the gains among a string of beneficiaries.*

Fighting the ATO on the front line are specialist firms like Arnold Bloch Leibler in Sydney. The company's infamous partner, Mark Leibler, is well-known in *"tax-avoidance elite"* circles as the brains behind hatching custom-made tax schemes for his many millionaire clients and multinational companies. (Leibler is also the man behind the Australia/Israel review an extremist Zionist Jewish publication which, in 1998, published the names and suburbs of 2,000 One Nation members under the heading *"Gotcha"*.)

On 2nd December 1998, the Coalition Government tabled its tax reform Bills. The legislation formerly introduced the Goods and Services Tax Bill of 1998 (GST) - a Bill which presents a classic example of deliberately missing the target. It is widely accepted that the people who will be most hurt by this new tax will be the poor and the elderly while the wealthy will remain largely unaffected. The issues of multinationals paying no tax is completely overlooked in the proposed tax changes.

The issues:

The overriding issue here is equity. While the newspapers are full of exposes on petty convicts and law breakers the main game is played behind closed doors in a game of *"cat and mouse"* with the tax office.

In recent years both media proprietors, the Murdoch and the Packer families, have been the subject of failed ATO investigations. They have used expensive and highly specialised tax lawyers to skirt around the issue of paying an equitable share of tax using the shambles represented by conflicting clauses in 30,000 pages of unworkable tax legislation.

With each success in the courts, based on this legislation supporting the tax system, the tax burden continues to shift from the rich and the multinationals onto the poor. The GST is, in many ways, nothing more than a new form of enforceable revenue raising by the government to stop-gap the flow of tax away from wealthy targets too hard to catch.

What is worse is the reality that the attraction of off-shore tax free havens to multinationals has resulted in the unfettered transfer of profits from Australia – with the resulting lack of ongoing investment adding to the country's employment woes.

What the major parties think about this issue:

The Labor Party's position about the GST is clear (even though Paul Keating wanted to introduce this tax in the 1980s).

Today the party says,

Tax And Big Business

It (the GST) is intrinsically regressive; because low-income families spend a much greater proportion of their total income than do high-income families, a GST imposes a higher tax rate on low-income than high income families. Furthermore, Treasurer Costello wants to broaden the indirect tax base and reduce indirect tax rates. Such a change would shift the burden of indirect tax from luxuries and discretionary durables, to everyday necessities, increasing the tax paid by ordinary working families and reducing the tax paid by high-income buyers of luxury goods.

Both the Labor Party and the Coalition have promised to close the tax loopholes used by the rich – but neither have. In fact, as can be seen in the background information both have been instrumental in providing the mega-rich with a myriad of unconscionable tax loopholes.

It is interesting to note that before gaining power in 1996 then opposition Treasurer Peter Costello promised to raise Au$800 million in lost taxes by targeting the wealthiest 100 families in Australia. Of course, once the Coalition got into government this idea was quickly shelved.

How the media have reported on this issue:

The mainstream media have embraced the government's plans for a GST while labelling untested optional tax policies such as One Nation's 2% Easytax as *"fruitloop"* policy. The policy decisions by consecutive Labor and Coalition governments which have added to the complex tax laws and provided loopholes remains one of the most unreported issues in the mainstream media.

The fact that 58% of companies in Australia pay no tax is not worth a mention.

Is there a solution:

The simple solution is to completely redraft the tax laws and close all the loopholes. This would have to include the removal of the attraction of tax avoidance options like off-shore tax havens and international transfer pricing arrangements.

Policies like the 2% Easytax or Debit Tax might not be the answer but at least it provides people with an alternative starting point to consider when returning equity back into taxation.

Chapter 16
The Two Party System And Compulsory Preferential Voting

Background:

It was the two party system which ensured that just under 10% of the Australian population today have absolutely no representation in the House of Representatives and just one Senator-elect, Heather Hill, in the Senate. Pauline Hanson's One Nation party was politically *"gang-banged"* by the political parties and the media in the lead-up to the October 1998 Federal Elections.

Traditionally the Liberal/National Coalition have alternated power sharing with the Labor Party. Many believe, with some justification, that both represent factions of the same power brokers – big business.

In the 1998 Federal Election Australia's third largest party, One Nation, did not receive one cent from big business. Its anti-globalisation policies would not benefit them. The book *"Murder by Media"* provides a terrifying insight into how the Australian media abused the very basics of ethical reporting to discredit the party. It details how the new kid on the block was derided by the political parties as *"racist"* and *"bigoted"* as they attempted to shore up their voter base which the polls said was draining away from them. How the Murdoch and Packer media empires' collusion resulted in a very effective campaign of political vilification against the newcomer. Top rating television programmes like *60 Minutes* with its *"Call to Arms"* segment and biased feature articles like *The Sydney Morning Herald's "The First Eleven"* were run ridiculing the party in the lead up to state and federal elections. Both examples cited above lacked ethics but gave the political parties good cover for presenting an argument to the nation to *"put One Nation last"* on the how-to-vote ticket.

The importance of the how-to-vote card under the current compulsory preferential voting system in the federal elections cannot be underestimated. It is recognised by the media.

In the critical weeks leading up to the Queensland State Election in June 1998 Murdoch's *The Courier-Mail* virtually forced the Liberal Party to revoke its decision to put One Nation above the Labor Party on its how-to-vote card.

The paper did this by running an astounding *three separate opinion pieces* in one week slamming the Liberal party and calling it *"pragmatic"* for even considering putting One Nation above the Labor party on the how-to-vote cards. The articles were written in the knowledge that the Liberal party was to hold a meeting to re-consider the allocation of preferences at the end of that week because of the media-outcry to an earlier decision to put One nation above Labor.

Shell-shocked by the adverse publicity the Liberal party backed down and agreed to allow individual candidates to put Labor above One Nation is they wished. Only one candidate, an Asian, did.

The Labor party had earlier claimed the *"moral high ground"* by putting One Nation last on all their how-to-vote cards. Consider the hypocrisy - Labor put a candidate for the *Nazi party* ahead of the Liberals in an earlier election – just to ensure that the Coalition had the worst possible chance of getting votes. You can now assess for yourself the concern that the Laboral factions had about the votes that One Nation was taking from its collective base.

The issues:

Compulsory Preferential Voting enforces the two party system – it takes away the opportunity for proportional representation by the people. The 1998 Federal Election result is a classic example of that.

Even in Pauline Hanson's seat of Blair the system defeated her – even though she gained more than double the primary votes received by the eventual winner, Cameron Thompson, who represented the Liberal Party.

Ms Hanson's vote rose from a primary count of 37% rose to about 47% while Thompson's primary count of just 17% jumped to 53% after preferences as the majority of the voters obediently followed the *"how-to-vote"* cards.

The preferences of the National party flowed on to the Liberals despite the fact that the policies of One Nation best represented the traditional National voter – consider, for example, the renewed push by the Coalition for the sale of Telstra.

What the major parties think about this issue:

The major parties have embraced compulsory preferential voting. The manner in which they traded preferences ahead of One Nation for *"moral reasons"* decries the truth. They will do anything to keep newcomers out of the picture.

The rushing through of a Bill late at night outlawing the *"Langer"* voting system just before the October 1998 Federal election removed the democratic option of only selecting parties that a voter supported when allocating preferences. If the voter did not number every box in a logical numerical format his vote was treated as invalid – shoring up the two party system.

The bi-lateral status quo had to be maintained at any costs. This required that the growing support for *"populist-based"* One Nation be stifled by each putting the other ahead of One Nation.

How the media have reported on this issue:

The direct involvement of the mainstream media in manipulating and pressurising the major parties for reasons of *"media-spun morality"* has got to be seen in the light of the clear hypocrisy of their actions.

In the lead up to the October 1998 Federal Election one man, Lachlan Murdoch, instructed his editors to *"Kill the cow"*... in other words destroy the political ambitions of Pauline Hanson. Much of the damage had already been inflicted by the manner in which the media interfered in the political process when it came to preferences.

Recorded below are extracts from three separate articles carried by Murdoch's *Courier-Mail* at a critical stage when the Liberal Party were deciding on how to distribute their preferences in the lead up to the June 1998 Queensland State Elections:

1. Opinion piece by Terry Sweetman[52], *Courier-Mail*, Tuesday, May 5th 1998:

Any doubts that the Queensland Liberal Party was something of a curious misnomer appear to have been settled by its weekend decision to direct preferences to Pauline Hanson's One Nation ahead of the Labor Party. And its continued failure to carve out a separate and distinctive identity for itself eventually could consign it to the ranks of historical curiosity.

The decision to direct preferences to Hanson's troglodytes is another indication that the Liberals are in bad shape politically, intellectually and, now, morally. The lame justification from state

---

[52] http://www.gwb.com.au/gwb/news/onenation/press/sweet1.html

president Bob Carroll was that his party was in the business of winning elections, not giving 'free kicks' to Labor.

2. Editorial, *Courier-Mail*[53], Wednesday, May 6th 1998:

For One Nation to hold or share the balance of power in a Queensland Parliament would be a victory for short-sighted and crude populism and an indictment of the major parties for allowing such a profound increase in public cynicism and disconnection with mainstream politics. This week's announcement by the Queensland Liberals that One Nation will receive preferences ahead of Labor will feed this disconnection. It is just the kind of political pragmatism over principle that drives voters to disillusionment."

3. Opinion piece by Wallace Brown[54], Friday May 8th 1998:

Yet any decision by the Liberals, and presumably the Nationals, to allocate preferences to One Nation candidates is bizarre. This conclusion may mot be conventional wisdom but it is bizarre precisely because it is not pragmatic. And it is not pragmatic because to give Hanson preferences is to give her credibility.

Just as the opinion polls had her withering on the vine nationally; just as she was disappearing from our television screens; just as more voters were beginning to realise that she had no real answers to her rhetoric and simplistic questions; just as some of the beat-up merchants on radio talk-back shows were starting to forget her; just as Premier Rob Borbidge and Queensland Liberal leader Joan Sheldon were insisting that Hanson was no problem – what happens? The Liberals themselves give her this boost.

On Friday 8th May the Liberal Party held a special meeting to discuss the preferences issue. Caving in to the intense media pressure it was intimidated into changing its official position of putting last its traditional enemy – Labor. The Liberal Party released the following statement:

Traditionally the Labor Party has been placed last on Liberal Party "How to Vote" cards. At this election, the distribution of preferences will be undertaken on a seat-by-seat basis when all candidates are known. This will be done in consultation with local campaign committees.

On the next day, 9th May 1998, state political writer John Lehmann wrote[55]:

---

[53] http://www.gwb.com.au/gwb/news/onenation/press/coredit3.html
[54] http://www.gwb.com.au/gwb/news/onenation/press/coredit4.html

Now, as the Liberals prepare for a difficult state election, they have effectively aligned themselves with their volatile creation in last-ditch bid to win back Hanson's followers and save their political hides.

Call it pragmatism, call it blatant hypocrisy - either way, Liberal state president Bob Carroll's push to deliver preferences to One Nation ahead of Labor will be perceived by many voters as a latent acceptance of Hanson's populism.

Whether this strategy will draw more voters back or push more away is debatable but the move is clear evidence the Coalition is fearful of One Nation's potential impact on its re-election bid.

Former Liberal Senator and Aboriginal elder Neville Bonner described it as repugnant; party stalwart Sir James Killen claimed an alien philosophy had evolved; state minister Bruce Davidson indicated a preference for Nazi party candidates over Labor; recently resigned Liberal MP John Bradford said the party was shamelessly adopting the Graham Richardson motto: "Whatever it takes".

When the preference issue was being decided by the Federal Coalition *The Courier-Mail*[56] wrote on the 11th September 1998:

The failure of the Prime Minister and the Deputy Prime Minister to insist that Liberal and National candidates must put One Nation last on their preference lists will increasingly haunt them over the next few weeks. Already it appears certain that several National MPs and candidates in Queensland and New South Wales will effectively give their preferences to One Nation, by putting One Nation candidates above the ALP. They argue the ALP is the "enemy" not One Nation. They are wrong....

It was different in the Queensland election, where it [One Nation] benefited from National and Liberal preferences. It failed to attract official preferences from those parties federally because of its perceived extremism. Its policies were regarded as so far beyond the pale, that, as occurred in the Queensland election, the Liberals would have suffered primary losses if they or their Coalition partners had given their preferences to One Nation.

After the election in an editorial[57] on the 9th October 1998 *The Courier-Mail* rejected the charge that the major parties had been

---

[55] http://www.gwb.com.au/gwb/news/onenation/press/coredit5.html

[56] http://www.geocities.com/CapitolHill/Senate/8789/coredit16.html

[57] http://www.geocities.com/CapitolHill/Senate/8789/couroff1.html

influenced by Murdoch's self-interest in conspiring to put One Nation last:

The answer for One Nation rests not with railing against the system, but in becoming part of it. It will only attract preferences if it can demonstrate that it is not a racist and reactionary party. It needs to show that it has well-considered policies. While it will attract a significant number of primary votes by relying on prejudices and anti-establishment sentiments, it will only attract preferences if it can prove to one or more established parties that it is part of the mainstream of political life in Australia.

In other words One Nation should stop rocking the boat - the boat in which the major parties and the media barons run Australia aided by unelected, paid political powerbrokers like Graham Richardson, Grahame Morris and Michael Kroger.

2UE Radio personality Alan Jones summed up the situation on the 6th October 1998, just three days after the Federal Election,[58]:

"Mr Beazley believes that because he outpolled the Liberals he has some sort of 'mandate' to oppose even though he didn't win government. What mandate then does One Nation have? The Democrats are saying that they have a mandate to oppose a GST in the Senate and indeed they won on Saturday night at least three and perhaps four seats in the Senate, yet they again won fewer votes for the Senate than did One Nation.

"At close of counting on Saturday night the Democrats had about 747,000 votes for the Senate across the country while One Nation had about 777,000.

"So if Mr Beazley's definition of mandate based on votes won as opposed to seats gained is to be valid across the board what mandate does One Nation have with more votes then both the National party and the Democrats.

Is there a solution:

The best and only democratic outcome is to allow optional preferential voting.

The law rushed through just before the October 1998 federal election outlawing the until then valid *"Langer method[59]"* of

---

[58] http://www.gwb.com.au/gwb/news/onenation/press/ajones9.html

[59] The Langer method involved putting a 1, then 2 then numbering all other boxes 3 – nullifying any preferences after "2".

preferential voting closed the final loophole for any voter not wanting to give the major parties a vote.

Optional preferential voting will allow any voter to choose whether or not he or she *wants to* distribute second, third, fourth preferences and so on.

The current compulsory preferential voting system has provided the major parties with a practically fool-proof control over government.

No matter how much an Australian voter dislikes the Liberal/National/Labor parties as their preferences are exhausted their vote eventually gets counted by one of the major parties – and subsequently proclaimed as *"support for their policies"*. To buck the system by not *"numbering every box"* results in that vote being discarded as null and void.

This is a crazy and undemocratic voting methodology which supports the policies of big business enacted through committees in Canberra while the Laboral factions joist like knights of old in parliament over their enactment.

The bottom-line is that the Laboral factions are pushing Australia towards a submissive role in a world ruled by corporations. Australians, for the sake of their children cannot allow this to happen.

Chapter 17
Un(der)employment

> *The ability of governments to use investment policy as a tool to promote social, economic and environmental goals will be forbidden under the MAI.*
> Tony Clarke, Polaris Institute

Background:

Prime Minister John Howard talks about *"freeing the labour market"* to create employment. Just what does he mean? Deregulating – removal of awards – think of the Vietnamese.

This is what Australian-based Phillips Fox, a large legal firm, wrote to me from their Hanoi office when I enquired about establishing a man-power intensive business in Vietnam:

Dear Mr Scott Balson[60]*,*

Doing Business in Vietnam

I am sorry for not being able to reply to you earlier. Following is a brief outline on some Vietnamese labour issues you queried in your e-mail message of 2 November 1998.

1. Costs of labour: Vietnam has a low minimum wage and a young, eager-to-learn workforce. However, foreign businesses are finding some of the labour compliance requirements restrictive, onerous and confusing.

The salary of an employee must be specified in his/her labour contract. It should be noted that salaries of Vietnamese employees must be expressed (in their labour contracts) in United States Dollars (US$). However, payments of such salaries must be made in Vietnamese Dong (VND) at the average exchange rate between the actual selling and purchase rates of the foreign currency inter-bank market published by the State Bank at the time of payment. At present, US$1 is approximately equal to VND14,000.

Minimum wages for several different categories of employment are published by the Ministry of Labour, War Invalids and Social Affairs. At present, the minimum wage for unskilled employees is US$45 per month in Hanoi and Ho Chi Minh City and US$30 - 40 elsewhere.

---

[60] http://www.gwb.com.au/gwb/news/498/0512.html

2. Ages of labour: So far, an employee must be a person of at least fifteen (15) years of age who is able to work and has entered into a labour contract.

I hope our answers satisfy your queries. Please do not hesitate to contact us if we can be of any further assistance.

Yours sincerely,

Truong Bich Lien, Legal Assistant, Phillips Fox, Hanoi Branch

The real impact of globalisation is summed up Alan Jones who said on the 16th December 1998[61]:

"All too simple of course for bureaucrats and politicians to even contemplate but just by way of interest I had a letter bloke who runs a ribbon company. They manufacture ribbons. These sorts of companies are being run out of town by imports often the product of labour which is paid for in some foreign country at the rate of 25 cents an hour.

"This bloke told me that imported ready to use ribbons to the year June 30 totalled 3.2 million. Their value? Au$26.5 million. My correspondent made the sensible point that that translated into about .... 100 direct jobs for Australians."

The reason that Australian business is moving offshore comes down to one word – profit. Now there is nothing wrong with making profits but when you remove protectionist trade tariffs, like Australia has, you allow big business to re-locate to countries where labour are paid little more than the slaves of old.

This profit-based move comes at a cost to tens of thousands of Australian jobs where people are paid more because of the higher standards of living in this country. The sting comes when the goods, once manufactured in Australia, are now imported tariff free – adding to our foreign debt.

The reason trade tariffs were introduced before the Lima agreement, *"globalisation"* and *"economic rationalism"* came in vogue was to protect the standard of living of all Australians.

The removal of trade tariffs, the push for privatisation of public utilities and economic rationalism are the major forces behind the high unemployment in this country today. All are aimed at bringing Australia into the so-called *"global economy"* – a world where the standard of living of most Australians will fall dramatically as the multinationals move their businesses to any country offering their shareholders the *"best deal"*.

---

[61] http://www.gwb.com.au/gwb/news/onenation/press/ajones13.html

Un(der)employment

The Age newspaper warned Australians in December 1997 that the need for industry to re-locate might be passing with a chicken factory attempting to employ Korean workers in Australia under work visas on half the salaries being demanded by their Australian counterparts. In the US the arrival of migrants from impoverished countries has already had a dramatic impact on the average earnings of males. The average hourly wage (in constant 1995 $) has dropped from $12.22 in 1979 to just $8.92 in 1995.

Many multinationals have their base in the US. When we think of the US we think of a rich nation where the majority of people are employed and happy. Noam Chomsky portrays a very different picture in his book "The Free Market Myth",

The US has the worst record of poverty in the industrialised world – a poverty level which is twice as high as England, which has the second worst record in the industrialised world. Tens of millions of people are hungry every night, including millions of children who are suffering from Third World levels of diseases and malnutrition. In New York City, the richest city in the world, 40% of children live below the poverty line, meaning essentially below the subsistence level, deprived of minimal conditions that offer some hope for escape from misery and destitution and violence..

The ILO (International Labor Organisation) has just published a report estimating the level of global unemployment – understood to mean the position of not having enough work for subsistence – in January 1994 at 30%. That, it says accurately, is a crisis worse than the 1930s. It is, moreover, just one part of a general worldwide human rights catastrophe. UNESCO estimates that about 500,000 children die every year from debt repayment alone... Meanwhile, the World Health Organisation (WHO) estimates that 11 million children die every year from easily treatable diseases. WHO's head calls it silent genocide.

People are working longer for less money. The workload is continuing to increase, while wages are continuing to decline – which is unprecedented for a recovery. US wages – as measured by labour costs per unit output – are now the lowest in the industrialised world apart from Britain.

In the US you see huge urban slums which are basically concentration camps which try to coop up superfluous people expecting them to prey on one another. If you can't coop them in slums then they'll have to go off to prison. In fact the prison rate has shot up and is by far the highest per capita rate in the industrialised world. It may be symbolic that a couple of days after the NAFTA vote the Senate passed a very ominous crime bill calling for 100,000 new police, high security regional prisons, boot camps for young offenders, extension of the death penalty and harsher sentencing, as well as other onerous measures."

When you consider that we are *"importing"* the unsociable work ethic of the multinationals it does not take much to realise that the Australian workforce will be heading down the same road that has been a dead-end to tens of millions of American citizens before.

Without employment at a fair wage and with McJobs now the norm we can no longer be the lucky country. That ideal once bandied about is now but a dream of days long gone.

The issues:

In the 1960s and 1970s when Australia was the *"lucky country"* the population could gain employment and a comfortable lifestyle without any problem at all. The *"Australian dream"* - home ownership – was obtainable to practically every adult in the country and unemployment was, to all intents and purposes, non-existent.

In the 1980s the Labor government started eroding the financial foundation supporting this idyllic lifestyle. Globalisation and economic rationalism started entering the Australian workplace under the Hawke and Keating leadership eating away like parasites.

As the multinationals took more and more of the wealth out of the country those employed in traditional jobs in areas such as banking and family farming became unemployed overnight.

With trade tariffs being removed our labour force is now at the mercy of the *"level playing field"* with our standard of living and our chances of gaining employment being the big losers.

What the major parties think about this issue:

The major parties always jump on to the *"jobs, jobs, jobs"* bandwagon at election time.

A recent classic case of political hypocrisy was the leader of the opposition Labor's Peter Beattie now Queensland State Premier who appeared to only know one word when in front of a television camera in the lead up to the state elections.

And that word was *"jobs"*.

"My government is about jobs," he would repeat with boring predictability, *"jobs, jobs, jobs."* Night after night in the lead up to voting day.

Un(der)employment

After he gained power his government quickly adopted the economic rationalist policies that were being pushed along by the Coalition before him.

One of the first victims of the new *"jobs, jobs, jobs"* Beattie government was publicly owned Suncorp/Metway. The organisation was Queensland's largest and last publicly owned financial organisation. In the lead up to the election Premier Beattie and his new Treasurer David Hamill had promised to *"stop the proposed sell-off of Suncorp/Metway in its tracks if elected to government"*.

The triple-whammy of the globalistic Hilmer report, National Competition Policy and the FSIA struck down once again with the new Labor government taking just a few weeks to embrace economic rationalism and allow the sale of Suncorp/Metway to go ahead despite its pre-election promises. The day after the Au$1.5 billion sale the price of the company's shares rose 40% on the market – revealing an undervaluation of about Au$600 million – *lost forever to the public of Queensland.*

Today the new Suncorp/Metway has embarked on the predictable rationalisation of closing branches and retrenching staff – in direct conflict to Beattie's promise to create *"jobs, jobs, jobs"*.

Beattie is not alone. One of the most savage proponents for privatisation has been Victoria's Premier Jeff Kennett. Practically everything in Victoria has been privatised and with the privatisation has come retrenchment and lower salaries.

The systemic destruction of hundreds of thousands of Australian jobs has been orchestrated by bureaucrats, international plureaucrats and governments at all levels over the last twenty years.

The Labor party's official position on employment is as follows:

Labor recognises that the fundamental objective of economic policy is to promote the well-being and improve the quality of life of all Australians: to improve living standards by providing maximum employment opportunity and rising incomes, and to enable the community to provide a decent standard of living for those unable to provide for themselves. Labor's better plan for the economy is aimed at achieving these objectives.

With abundant natural and human resources, Australia is better equipped than most countries to pursue and achieve this fundamental objective. Other objectives of economic policy, including controlling inflation and reducing current account ι eficits, are not ends in themselves, but means to the achievement of the fundamental objective of higher living standards.

Good economic policy puts people first, matching competence and efficiency with compassion and care. Labor is committed to achieving full employment, meaning that anyone who wants a job can find one within a reasonable time. Employment and employment security are the keys to personal and social well-being: to stable relationships and family life, and access to the necessities and pleasures of life.

Unemployment, underemployment and widespread job insecurity are all profoundly debilitating for individuals and communities. Everyone capable of employment should be able to secure a job, education or training: unemployment is not an acceptable option.

However difficult full employment may be to achieve in the short to medium term, Labor will always pursue this as our highest priority objective.

Perhaps the recent *moving of employment* from the old Department of Employment, Education and Training (DEET) (now known as the Department of Education, Training and Youth Affairs) to the Department of Employment, Workplace Relations and Small Business (DEWSB) says something about the Coalition government's real interest in solving the employment problem in Australia.

DEWSB state that,

The female labour force participation rate (trend series) has risen by 10 percentage points, from 43.7% in May 1978 to 53.7% in May 1997. Over the same period the labour force participation rate for married females rose even more strongly, from 41.7% to 54.9%. A continuation of this trend is likely to increase the demand for formal child care. It should be noted, however, that the rate of usage of long day care services for non work-related purposes has also been increasing.

The need for both partners to work is an obvious outcome when salaries and standards of living fall.

How the media have reported on this issue:

The mainstream media has presented the picture that unemployment is now falling under the Coalition. They have never really taken the government (both Laboral factions) to task about *underemployment*.

The fact that people are now being force salaries is ignored with the papers proudly proclaim inflation rate has dropped to nearly 0. What is not reported while the rich continue to grow richer the growing number of people below the poverty line in Australia grow poorer – shoring up the resulting inequitable balance in the inflation rate.

One of the earliest signals of the rise of slums in Australia is the fall in property prices in low income areas with the contrary explosion of prices in the richer suburbs. We are looking at the very early stages of regional slums in Australia – now a common social reality in America.

Is there a solution:

The solution is built around drastically reclaiming Australia for ourselves.

There is very little of value in this country still in Australian hands – and despite the promise of a resulting brighter future the reverse has actually been the case.

The manner in which the bureaucrats have led Australia into the *"globalised"* world and the manner in which the people's representatives have danced to their tune reflects a very sick political system.

Unless this is changed and the people regain their control over their public assets unemployment will rise in the foreseeable future and the standards of living for most Australians continue to drop dramatically.

The media would have us believe that we should push on bravely into the 21st Century under the *"unstoppable"* banner of globalisation. To have a contrary thought is to be seen by this big business industry as being backward and simplistic.

The Colonisation of the world under corporate rule is so far advanced today that the only thing missing from the puzzle is global government and many believe that that is not far away.

Our children might question one day how we could let this happen, or more likely, never be allowed to know that it did.

The new age slaves live in a world that we allowed to evolve.

God save them and us, because our politicians won't.